Snarky as F*ck

Snarky as F*ck

A Sassy, Irreverent Guide for Dealing with People's Bullsh*t

Lawrence Dorfman

Skyhorse Publishing

Skyhorse Publishing books may be purchased in bulk at special discounts for sales promotion, corporate gifts, fund-raising, or educational purposes. Special editions can also be created to specifications. For details, contact the Special Sales Department, Skyhorse Publishing, 307 West 36th Street, 11th Floor, New York, NY 10018 or info@skyhorsepublishing.com.

Skyhorse® and Skyhorse Publishing® are registered trademarks of Skyhorse Publishing, Inc.®, a Delaware corporation.

Visit our website at www.skyhorsepublishing.com.

Please follow our publisher Tony Lyons on Instagram @tonylyonsisuncertain

10 9 8 7 6 5 4 3 2 1

Library of Congress Cataloging-in-Publication Data is available on file.

Cover design by Kai Texel
Cover artwork by Getty Images

Print ISBN: 978-1-5107-7783-5
Ebook ISBN: 978-1-5107-7887-0

Printed in China

CONTENTS

INTRODUCTION:

Punching People in the Face with Your Words

When I was a kid, every time I said good night to my dad, I'd say, "I'll see you later." He always replied, "Not if I see you first." It took me years and years to understand the snark of that response. Essentially, he was insinuating that if he did see me first, he was going to run the other way. What a shit! (He's also the dickhead who loved telling me to take a long walk off a short pier.)

Now, even as an old fart, Dad's a smart guy. He's also always passive-aggressively pissed off, with a few interludes of simply aggressively pissed off. And he's funny. To, me, these attributes are necessary ingredients for an awesome snark sandwich: intelligence, wit, passive-aggressiveness, with a dash of anger. (*I'll also throw in "insecurity," because, ultimately, I hope Dad reads this and gets pissed.*)

At its best, snark is a friendly bit of sarcastic banter between friends. At its even bester, it's like punching someone in the face with your words. And in this book— we have both kinds of snark, because we want you to be happy with this purchase. (*And if you're not, it's most likely your fault.*) Whether a witty comeback, a well-turned line, a pithy bon mot, a great retort, a cut-to-the-quick insult, or a clever retort, this book has got you covered.

From sex and romance (*not necessarily in that order*) to things you wish you could say to your boss, from idiots who use social media to family and friends (*many times one and the same*), we've got the snarky stuff you want.

Here are a few things in this book:

+ Sick burns
+ Greeting cards from Snarkville
+ Snarky movie reviews
+ Snarky responses to people DMing unwanted dick pics
+ The Snark Hall of Fame (full of quotes from real and imagined people)

Here are a few things not in this book:

+ "Take my wife, please" jokes. (*Ha, ha, we get it, wives are annoying, and husbands are lazy! The twenty-first century has a lot more going on than these sorts of outdated gender clichés!*)

+ Anything that might feel like we are punching down. (*In fact, as part of our definition of snark, we'd like to include that being snarky is a lot like punching upward, or at least laterally. So, who's lateral? Your co-worker. That guy ahead of you at the grocery store who says, "Hold my place. I forgot the ketchup." Your book editor, who is waiting for those rewrites. The shirtless Facebook profile picture guy. Internet idiots. And yes, even your boss—because most likely, he or she is a shlep just like us.*)

So, what are you waiting for? Buy this book for your bitter friends. Bring it to the work party your partner is forcing you to go to. Slip it into someone's bathroom, where it will be read for years to come ... or until someone decides to clean. *(Caution: These pages are not flushable.)*

You'll laugh. You'll cry. You'll laugh so hard that you're crying. And vice versa.

Ready?

"Sarcasm is weird. Even not in acting, in life I feel 'sarcastic' is a word that people use to describe me sometimes, so when I meet someone, it's almost they feel they have to also be sarcastic, but it can sometimes just come off as mean if it's not used in the right way."

—AUBREY PLAZA

CHAPTER ONE:

Sex(ting)
and
(Online) Romance

We try out new pick-up lines with our dates online. We swipe one way or the other online. We have sex online. We ghost each other online. We slip into their DMs, like their stupid fucking updates, tweets, texts, etc. etc. The one thing we never seem to do is actually meet. Sure it saves on flowers and meals, costly STD cures, and raising children, but does anyone else miss the good old days when people met at church gatherings and county fairs? Okay, sure, the "old days" was more like waking up after a bender with a stranger in your bed (is it your bed or someone else's?), what feels like sandpaper in your mouth (it used to be your tongue), and your clothes god knows where . . . but you get the drift.

Let the snarks fly!

As Sylvia lay on her deathbed, she beckoned her husband of forty years to her side.

"Robert," she said, "When I die I want you to marry Mary."

"Mary? I thought you hated her?"

"I do."

✦✦✦

I wish I were cross-eyed so I could see you twice.

✦✦✦

The patient lies back on the examination table, clothes on the floor, and says, "Kiss me, Doctor."

"No I can't," replies the doctor.

"Oh go on, kiss me, kiss me," the patient insists.

"No it's out of the question," says the doctor.

"But why?" The patient asks.

"Well, it's completely against ethics rules," the doctor replies. "In fact, strictly speaking, I shouldn't even be having sex with you."

There's a giant sale at my
place tonight.
All clothes are 100% off.

♦♦♦

Lady Nancy Astor once got annoyed at Winston
Churchill.
"Winston," she said sharply, "if you were my
husband I'd put poison in your coffee."
"And if I were your husband," responded
Churchill, "I'd drink it."

♦♦♦

"My wife just had a baby!"
"Congratulations! Whose is it?"

Doctor: Do you exercise?
Patient: Does sex count?
Doctor: Yes.
Patient: Then, no.

What does Pinocchio's lover
say to him?
Lie to me! Lie to me!

If you had to choose between true
love and traveling the world, which
country would you choose first?

**Why does Santa have a big sack?
He only comes once a year.**

Dog Blocking: When the dog prevents
you from having sex by lying between you
and your partner.

Q: Why do walruses love a Tupperware
   party?
A: They're always looking for a tight
   seal.

When her husband passed away, a woman put the usual death notice in the newspaper, but added that he had died of gonorrhea.

Once the daily newspapers had been delivered, a good friend of the family phoned and complained bitterly, "You know very well that he died of diarrhea, not gonorrhea." Replied the widow, "Yes, I know that he died of diarrhea, but I thought it would be better for posterity to remember him as a great lover rather than the big shit that he really was."

Q: The difference between savings bonds and men?

A: At some point, bonds mature.

Q: "Are you a single parent?"
A: "No."

Q: "Would you like to be?"
A: _____

A woman goes to a doctor complaining about knee pains. "Do you indulge in any activities that puts pressure on your knees?" asks the doctor. "Well, my husband and I do it doggy style every night."

"I see," said the doctor.

"You know, there are other sexual positions."

"Not if you want to watch TV, there ain't."

Q: What's the difference between a bar and a clitoris?

A: Most men have no trouble finding a bar.

Q: What's the difference between kinky and perverted?

A: Kinky is when you tickle your partner with a feather. Perverted is when you use the whole bird.

Q: Does Viagra work.

A: Yes, it does!

Q: Can you get it over the counter?

A: If I take two.

A guy is sitting in the examination room. The doctor walks in and says, "I'm afraid you're going to have to stop masturbating."

"I don't understand, doc," the patient says. "Why?"

"Because," the doctor says, "I'm trying to examine you."

♦♦♦

Newsflash! Two men broke into a drugstore and stole all the Viagra. Be on the lookout for the two hardened criminals.

A really shy, introverted guy goes into a bar and sees a beautiful woman sitting at the bar. After an hour of gathering up his courage he finally goes over to her and asks, tentatively:

"Um, would you mind if I chatted with you for a while?"

She responds by yelling, at the top of her lungs, "No, I won't sleep with you tonight!"

Everyone in the bar is now staring at them. Naturally, the guy is hopelessly and completely embarrassed and he slinks back to his table. After a few minutes, the woman walks over to him and apologizes.

She smiles at him and says, "I'm sorry if I embarrassed you. You see, I'm a graduate student in psychology and I'm studying how people respond to embarrassing situations."

To which he responds, at the top of his lungs, "What do you mean $200?"

They Said It . . . Not Me

The only thing people like doing more than having sex is talking about sex.

∾

"The function of muscle is to pull and not to push, except in the case of the genitals and the tongue."
—LEONARDO DA VINCI

"There are four basic human needs; food, sleep, sex, and revenge."
—BANKSY

"It's the twenty-first century. I don't need an alpha male to protect me. I don't need a big, strong man to fight off a tiger. I need a geek who can get my naked photos off the cloud."
—WHITNEY CUMMINGS

"It's better to have a relationship with someone who cheats on you than someone who doesn't flush the toilet."
—UMA THURMAN

"Sex is not the answer. Sex is the question. 'Yes' is the answer."
—SWAMI X

"If I miss sex, I've got a drawer full of vibrators. All is good."
—JANE FONDA

"Have you ever dated a sex addict? At first, it's so much fun. You're like, 'Am I the hottest piece of ass in the world?' And then you're like, 'Oh, no. He would fuck a mailbox.'"
—AMY SCHUMER

"Women might be able to fake orgasms. But men can fake whole relationships."
—SHARON STONE

"He is every other inch a gentleman."
—REBECCA WEST

"There's nothing better than good sex . . . but bad sex? A peanut-butter-and-jelly sandwich is better than bad sex."
—BILLY JOEL

"I think we can all agree that sleeping around is a great way to meet people."
—CHELSEA HANDLER

"Going on a date tonight with $11 in my bank account. Let's hope he's not a feminist."
—RACHEL SENNOTT

"Physics is like sex: sure, it may give some practical results, but that's not why we do it."

—RICHARD P. FEYNMAN

•••

"Good sex is like good bridge. If you don't have a good partner, you'd better have a good hand."

—MAE WEST

Are You . . .

Pick-up lines are so cringe. Me saying "so cringe" is even cringier. Be that as it may, fuck pick-up lines already. We know you just looked up some up online, and if that's the best you can do, you're a lost cause. Give it up.

∽

French? Because Eiffel for you.
No, I'm Finnish. Finnish with this conversation.

✦✦✦

From Tennessee? Because you're the only 10 I see!
No, I'm from Fuckoff, because . . . fuck off.

A parking ticket? Because you've got "fine" written all over you.
No, I'm a "No Parking" sign—keep moving.

✦✦✦

Medusa? Because when I look at you, I get rock hard.
No, I'm just having a bad hair day. But it would be nice if you stopped looking at me already.

A bank loan? Because you got my interest.
No, I'm a teller, and my job is to teller you to leave me alone.

◆◆◆

A time traveler? Cause I see you in my future!
Yes, and I went back two hundred years into the past and found your pickup line.

◆◆◆

A magician? Because when I look at you, everyone else disappears.
Yes, in fact, and here's my vanishing act.

Tired? Because you've been running through my mind all night.
No, but I'll be tired later after running away from you.

◆◆◆

My appendix? Because I don't know what you do, but this feeling in my stomach makes me want to take you out.
No, I'm your brain, and it's apparently already been removed.

A beaver?
Cuz dam!
*No, I'm an otter—
as in, that pickup
line is otterly
awful.*

A broom? Because
you've swept me off
my feet.
*No, but you must be
a vacuum, because
you suck.*

A minivan? Because I want
you to carry my children.
*No, I'm a Porsche. I'm fast,
sexy, and too much for you
to handle.*

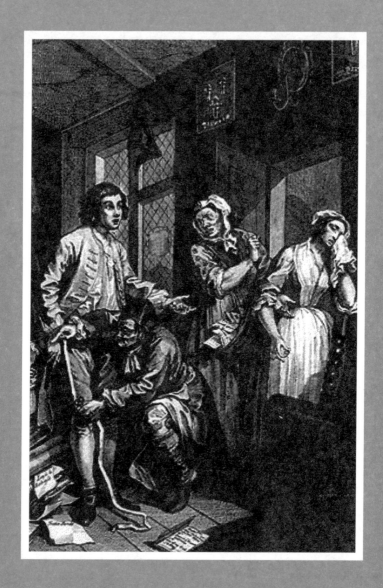

Snarky Dick Pic Responses

Okay, the real question here is whether or not there is such a thing as a *wanted* dick pic. Most of these assholes are putting the cart *waaaay* before the horse. If you are the recipient of one, try out one of these methods that will ensure it is the only one that guy sends you . . . or anyone else for that matter.

1. Circle a small spot on the dick and tell the guy he should get that checked out immediately. Include a link to WebMD.
2. Complain that your phone doesn't have a zoom function.
3. "LOL"
4. Say you're sorry you didn't get the picture because the file was too small.
5. "OMG, it's like a dick, but smaller."
6. "Oh, my! What happened?"
7. Rate it. 2 out of 10 should suffice.

8. "Oh, that reminds me, we're out of baby carrots."

9. Send an emoji that makes no fucking sense given the circumstances. Try the poop emoji, the hand that's either waving hello or goodbye, or the backgammon emoji. (Yes, there is a backgammon emoji.)

10. "You know, my late boyfriend had the same disease."

11. "My mom says she's seen better."

12. "Irreversible proof that you've got more dick in your personality than you have in your pants."

13. Send him back a random dick pic from online.

14. One word: Photoshop.

15. "Acting like a dick won't make yours any bigger."

16. Send a magnifying glass emoji.

17. Call it "cute."

18. Take a screen shot with the response, "hahahaha." Send it to him, and when he asks what's so funny, text, "Whoops, wrong person."

"Ladies: Don't come off desperate and reply quickly to your crushes texts. Wait a while. Meet someone else. Get married. Start a family. Keep him guessing."
—Violet K. Benson

✦✦✦

"I don't like eating bananas in public. That is so stressful if you're a girl. It's so annoying 'cause it's such a portable, good snack, but if you're a girl and you want to eat a banana all of a sudden you're in the position of like, how to I de-dick this delicious treat?"
—Chelsea Peretti

Punny Pick-up Lines

These pick-up lines are great if you want to send the message that you are harmless, basic, and do not want sex at all.

- If you were a chicken, you'd be impeccable.
- Life without you is like a broken pencil . . . pointless.
- Do you like *Star Wars?* Because Yoda only one for me!
- Hey, my name's Microsoft. Can I crash at your place tonight?
- Do you work at Starbucks, because I like you a latte?
- I bet you never use your left hand, because you are all right!
- Is your name Ariel? Because I think we mermaid for each other.

"On a scale of one to America, how free are you tonight?"
"North Korea."

"I would travel to the end of the world for you."
"But will you stay there?"

A study in the *Journal of Sex Research* claims men send dick pics in the hopes of receiving nudes in return or because they hope the pic leads to sex.

This study belongs with the one that claims going bald is upsetting and sword swallowing can be dangerous.

Excuses to Get Out of a Date

The next time someone you don't want to date asks you out, instead of being straightforward with them, use one of these lame excuses.

∿

I'm teaching my dog to yodel.

•••

I prefer to remain an enigma. Or a conundrum. I forget which.

•••

I need to refrigerate that new corpse.

Sorry, I'm trying to finish *He's Just Not That Into You.*

•••

I don't think you can afford the lifestyle I've become accustomed to.

•••

I'm so sorry but my shrink doesn't think you sound right for me.

Sorry, Netflix keeps playing the next episode before I can turn off the TV.

•••

I need to check in with my probation officer.

I left my toaster plugged in.

•••

Sorry, I have to go—I left my refrigerator running.

•••

I can't, I'm out of underwear.

Oh, Yay, You're Mansplaining

Mansplaining is a real thing. A 2008 essay by Rebecca Solnit defined mansplaining as "a man interrupting a woman to explain to her something that she actually knows more about than he does." Here are some suggested replies to mansplaining:

∾

"I'm sorry, what did you say? I have a terrible habit of ignoring people who bore me."

✦✦✦

"Thank you so much for explaining my own profession to me."

✦✦✦

"Your manslation really added to that discussion, buddy."

"You know, I have to agree with you that my having a uterus means I can't comprehend complex concepts."

+++

"That's a really interesting theory, but now let's hear from someone who actually has experience in this area."

+++

"It's impressive how much of this subject you know about without having any actual experience."

+++

"Remember when I asked for your opinion? Yeah me neither."

+++

"If a man is talking in the forest, and no woman is there to hear him, is he still wrong?"

Gross Couple

You know that couple that acts all cutesy to the point you want to vomit? They share gum, talk about smelling their pillow when they are apart, and giggle when one of them farts. Damn. Separately these two people were fun to be around, but now? Get me away from them. Or, even worse, are *you* in a gross couple relationship? Fuck, you'd better take this quiz and find out.

1. You have that app that tells you how far away your other half is from you.

                                        Yes or No

                    ✦✦✦

2. You count your anniversary by the week.

                                        Yes or No

3. Your background screen is a selfie of the two of you kissing.

Yes or No

+++

4. One asks to smell their armpit to check how stinky they are, and the other one does it.

Yes or No

+++

5. You post mushy gross statements about each other on social media.

Yes or No

+++

6. You wear themed Halloween costumes.

Yes or No

+++

7. In your contacts, your other half is named Baby or Boo with a thousand emojis

Yes or No

8. You feed each other . . . in public.

> Yes or No

◆◆◆

9. You talk to each other in baby voices.

> Yes or No

◆◆◆

10. Burped into each other's mouths to guess what you had for lunch.

> Yes or No

◆◆◆

Each Yes is worth one point. Score 0: You're barely a couple, actually; 1-3: Please, go elsewhere with that shit; 4-7: Get a room, and stay there; 8-10: You're going to get married, have three kids, and then cheat on each other when you both realize how much life you've wasted with each other.

Researchers from Ohio State University have found that gross couples are happier in their relationships and have more sex. *Honey, can you help me pop my back zit?*

Things You Don't Want to Hear During Sex

Beyond the old favorites, "That's never happened before" and "Can you make me a sandwich," there are plenty of other statements from your sexual partner you'd rather not hear . . . ever.

∽

Well, so much for mouth-to-mouth.

•••

Hope you're as good looking when I'm sober . . .

What's your Netflix password?

•••

I thought *you* had the keys to the handcuffs.

•••

Yes, dear, I'm awake.

Do you smell something burning?

•••

Can you please pass me the remote control?

•••

Yeah, on second thought, let's turn off the lights.

•••

But my cat always sleeps on that pillow.

Did I tell you my aunt died in this bed?

•••

No, really . . . I do this part better myself!

•••

This would be more fun with a few more people . . .

•••

So much for the fulfillment of sexual fantasies!

•••

I think you have it on backwards.

You're good enough to do this for a living!

✦✦✦

Is that blood on the headboard?

✦✦✦

Are you sure I don't know you from somewhere?

✦✦✦

Does this count as a date?

✦✦✦

Don't mind me, I always file my nails in bed.

I hope I didn't forget to turn the gas oven off. Do you have a light?

✦✦✦

You could at least act like you're enjoying it!

✦✦✦

You're almost as good as my ex!

✦✦✦

You look younger than you feel.

✦✦✦

Perhaps you're just out of practice.

And to think, I didn't even have to buy you dinner!

◆◆◆

I'd rather be waterboarding.

◆◆◆

I'll tell you who I'm fantasizing about if you tell me who you're fantasizing about . . .

◆◆◆

Keep it down . . . my mom is a light sleeper . . .

My old partner used to do it a lot longer!

◆◆◆

Twins can feel what's happening to each other, and mine just called to complain.

◆◆◆

Could we do this without kissing? I'm trying to make a call.

◆◆◆

I haven't felt this good since the conjugal visits.

Douchebag Pick-up Line Fill-in-the-Blanks

Pick-up lines should be used as douchebag indicators. Here are ten of the worst lines, and if you know more than five of these fill-in-the-blank answers, well then . . . we'll send your Official Douchebag starter kit within five business days.

∽

1. Do you believe in love at first sight—or should I _____?

2. Well, here I am! What are your other _____?

3. You're a 9 out of 10, and I'm the _____ you need.

4. I may not go down in history, but I'd definitely go
   _____.

5. You know what's funny? Before I came in here, I thought *I* was _____.

6. All those curves, and me with no _____.

7. You're hot. I'm ugly. Let's make _____ babies.

8. Don't worry, it only seems kinky the _____.

9. You're so fine, you make me want to go out and get a _____.

10. I would totally let you take me to _____.

Answers: 1. walk by again; 2. two wishes; 3. one; 4. down on you; 5. hot; 6. brakes; 7. average; 8. first time; 9. job; 10. brunch

You Know You're Dating a Grown-up if ♦ ♦ ♦

We all just want someone we can date without rolling our eyes so far back we see our brains, right!? Here are some ways to tell if you found someone ready to settle down with.

∾

They don't know when Mickey D's opens . . . or closes.

♦♦♦

They sure as hell don't call McDonalds "Mickey D's."

♦♦♦

They have houseplants, and none of them are smokeable.

♦♦♦

They hear their favorite song . . . in an elevator.

6:30 am is when they wake up . . . not when they go to sleep.

+++

Their friends no longer hook up . . . they get married.

+++

They no longer like their dog better than you.

+++

They're boring as fuck.

+++

What do you call a cheap circumcision?
A rip off.

Dating Site Tips

Hinge, Tinder, Bumble, oh my! Got FOBSL (fear of being swiped left)? Well then, don't do the following and you might have a chance.

∽

Don't start off the conversation talking about your genitals.
Really. It's not a good look.

✦✦✦

Only post photos with you wearing a shirt.
That goes for everyone.

✦✦✦

Don't brag about your TGI Fridays coupon.
Wait till your mom comes over to whip out that bad boy.

You know that favorite pick-up line of yours?
Yeah . . . so does everyone else.

✦✦✦

Stop it with all the things you are NOT looking
for in a partner.
Dating isn't à la carte, dumbass.

✦✦✦

Don't use pre-written conversation starters.
*People swiping one way or the other on you have the same
damn starters and now know you have not an original
thought in your head.*

✦✦✦

Don't write the person's name when messaging them.
Karen, it can get creepy, couldn't it, Karen?

✦✦✦

Don't call yourself an entrepreneur.
*We all know this means you are between jobs
at the moment.*

Dogs are great—no need to go on and on about them.
Nobody is here for the dog pics.

◆◆◆

Don't say you love music.
What the hell does that even mean!? That's like saying you're a big fan of oxygen.

◆◆◆

You're a lot like a microwave dinner. You're ready in three minutes, you look nothing like your photos, and you're just good enough for me to want you again when I'm desperate.

◆◆◆

What's the difference between you and your couch?
Your couch gets a lot more ass than you do

◆◆◆

What's another difference between you and your couch?
Your couch can support a family.

Emotional Damage!

Here are a few things to say when your partner or date
is being such a dick. These work at movies, during
dinner, or even when you're just hanging out. These are
meant to either stop shitty behavior or to get your date
to a quick end.

∾

You've got a "forty-divorced-not-allowed-to-see-the-kids"
vibe going on right now.

✦✦✦

You're not that lucky, and I'm not that desperate!

✦✦✦

You'd be in good shape if you ran as much as your mouth.

✦✦✦

You're the reason this country has to put directions on
shampoo and warning labels on plastic bags.

I'm sorry I hurt your feelings when I called you stupid. I really thought you already knew.

+++

I'm 97 percent sure you don't like me but I'm 100 percent sure I don't care.

+++

It's a beautiful day to leave me alone.

+++

Sure, I'll help you out . . . the same way you came in.

+++

Congratulations! You've managed to make me feel like a worthless piece of shit again. Would you like an award for that?

+++

You are the result of four billion years of evolution. Please act like it.

Dear . . .

Dear One Night Stand,
I don't mind that you left before I woke up, but you realize we were at *your* place, right!?

◆◆◆

Dear Future Husband,
I will never, ever be comfortable enough with you to pee with the door open. So, close the fucking door.

◆◆◆

Dear Future Wife,
I can't wait to spend so much quality time with you. Do you want to be on my Fantasy Football team?

◆◆◆

Dear Person I Ghosted,
. . .

Dear Me,

Whatever you do tonight, keep your dignity intact. Ooh, look! It's two for one margaritas tonight!

+++

Dear Mom and Dad,

You told me to never settle when it comes to love. Instead, I've followed your example, and you will be able to meet the person I've fallen in love with in three to six months.

+++

Dear Bumble Match,

I'm suspicious about your intentions. For instance, I wouldn't even settle for me, so why would you?

Demotivational Quotes About Love

Feeling down and out? Wishing that special person would show up and change your life forever? Yeah, sorry, this is a snark book, so good luck with that.

✦✦✦

"Never go to bed mad. Stay up and fight."
—Phyllis Diller

✦✦✦

There are plenty of fish in the sea; none of them want to date you either.

✦✦✦

True love is when two people lower their standards just the right amount.

Date someone who is too good for you and pray they never find out.

♦♦♦

"I'm going to stop pretending to have orgasms with you."
"That's great! I'll stop pretending that I care."

♦♦♦

Men are like pantyhose. They either run, cling, or don't fit right in the crotch.

♦♦♦

Don't call it making love. "Disappointing people" is more like it.

♦♦♦

Marriage isn't a word. It's a sentence.

♦♦♦

"In the beginning, love is mostly about lying to each other. It's like that in the end, too."
—Brian K. Vaughan

Married Sexting

Married? With children, mortgage, soccer practice, volleyball tournament, wait! Don't forget your lunch? Teaching you how to sext is probably going to be a lot like teaching our great-grandparents how to send an email, but we gotta start somewhere.

✦✦✦

Oh baby, I'm not wearing any underwear . . . *because you forgot to put the fucking clothes in the dryer.*

✦✦✦

I'm so hot for you.
Maybe it's menopause.

✦✦✦

Baby, I'll be home at 6 pm.
I'm leaving at 6:01. Make sure the kids are asleep before I get home.

I think tonight's a great night to bring home a bottle of wine . . . *and get yourself something for dinner, too.*

✦✦✦

Hey, baby, what's cooking?
It's when you heat up food to make them taste better. You should try it some time.

✦✦✦

Hey, sexy. I just shaved down there. You know what that means, right?
Yeah, the drain is clogged again.

✦✦✦

Do you want to watch porn or golf tonight?
Porn. You already know how to golf.

"If you made a list of the reasons why any couple got married, and another list of the reasons for their divorce, you'd have a hell of a lot of overlapping."
—MIGNON MCLAUGHLIN

◆◆◆

"They had no problem saying 'til death do you part' back then, because they didn't live that long. They had plagues, you know? Soon as that guy got on your nerves, here come some locusts to eat his ass up for you."
—WANDA SYKES

Types of Sex

SMURF SEX: The first throes of passion, when you're fucking until you're blue in the face.

+++

KITCHEN SEX: You're definitely a couple, but you're still attracted enough to be overcome with desire while making dinner. The counters are not off limits.

+++

BEDROOM SEX: Her thong has become a brief, he's wearing pajamas, and the sex happens in bed.

+++

RELIGIOUS SEX: Nun in the morning, nun in the afternoon, and nun at night.

HALLWAY SEX: You've been together too long. When you pass each other in the hallway, you say, "Fuck you."

✦✦✦

COURTROOM SEX: Your soon-to-be ex-wife and her lawyer screw you in divorce court in front of many people and for every penny you've got.

✦✦✦

SOCIAL SECURITY SEX: Back in the game, you now get a little each month. But it's not enough to live on.

Occupational Dating Hazards

Sometimes a person's job description doesn't exactly match what you're imagining when you're swiping away on your favorite dating site. Keep the following in mind:

∽

Plumber
Good: Knows all about couplings.
Bad: Just can't say no to crack.

✦✦✦

Food Inspector
Good: Knows all the good restaurants.
Bad: Is a food inspector.

✦✦✦

Entrepreneur
Good: Probably an outside-the-box-thinker.
Bad: Yeah, this person doesn't have a job.

Manager

Good: Expecting monumental growth.

Bad: Very used to downsizing.

+++

Weather Forecaster

Good: Makes bold predictions.

Bad: Is often wrong.

+++

Editor

Good: Knows just what to say to get you in the mood.

Bad: Copyedits your sexts.

+++

Elevator Operator

Good: Knows when to go down.

Bad: Only presses one button at a time.

A Dad
Good: Great with your kids.
Bad: Puns. All. The. Puns.

+++

A Mom
Good: Knows what you need before you do.
Bad: Is already raising three fucking kids and doesn't
need another one.

+++

A Mortician
Good: Will be the last person to ever let you down.
Bad: Will be the last person to ever let you down.

+++

Professional Skier
Good: At first, you're on top of the world.
Bad: It's all downhill after that.

"Yesterday my husband ran off with my best friend, Karen."
"Since when is Karen your best friend?"
"Since yesterday."

Love is grand; divorce is a hundred grand.

Q: How does the alchemist satisfy his wife?
A: Elixir.

"Love is only a dirty trick played on us to achieve continuation of the species."
—W. Somerset Maugham

CHAPTER TWO:

Where You At?: Snarky Geography

We are all so proud of where we come from (for no reason whatsoever). We celebrate our culture (boring), our food (it tastes like wood glue), and our hometown sports teams (0–17). Meanwhile, anyone not from our hometown thinks we are idiots. And we think they, in turn, are twats. All kidding aside, knowing our place in this world can help us develop a sense of who we truly are (assholes) and help us stay focused on the things that matter most to us (being assholes).

Q: What do they call one hundred John
   Deeres circling a McDonald's in Iowa?
A: Prom night.

Q: Did you hear about the guy from Indiana
   who died drinking milk?
A: Yeah, the cow fell on him.

Q: What do a jackknifed semi in Ohio, a
   guy getting a divorce in Alabama, and a
   tornado in Kansas have in common?
A: They're all fixin' to lose a trailer.

Q: Why are cowboys' hats turned up on the
   sides in Wyoming?
A: So that three people can fit in the pickup.

Q: What's the difference between Kansas and yogurt?
A: Yogurt has an active living culture.

It isn't necessary to have relatives in Kansas City in order to be unhappy.
—GROUCHO MARX

While fishing off the South Carolina coast, a New York tourist capsized his boat. He yelled to an old man standing on the shore, "Are there any gators around here?!" "Naw," the man yelled back, "They ain't been around for years!" The New Yorker started swimming toward shore. Halfway there, he asked the guy, "How'd you get rid of the gators?" "We didn't do nothing," the old guy said. "The sharks got 'em."

An Alaskan was on trial in Anchorage. The prosecutor leaned toward him and asked, "Where were you on the night of October to April?"

Philadelphia sunscreen: an empty sunscreen container used to smuggle alcohol into events.
A North Dakota seven-course meal: a hamburger and a six pack.

Chicago: Come for the deep-dish pizza. Stay because you got murdered.

Kansas Kleenex: holding one nostril closed while blowing snot out of the other.

They Said It . . . Not Me

Don't blame me for these not-so-kind takes on these places. Famous people said it, so hit them up on social media and tell they are wrong . . . or right.

"In America, anyone can become president.
That's the problem."
—GEORGE CARLIN

✦✦✦

"God created war so that Americans would learn geography."
—MARK TWAIN

✦✦✦

"I moved to New York City for my health. I'm paranoid, and it was the only place where my fears were justified."
—ANITA WEISS

"As you know, the bear hunting season in New Jersey is a little bit different. First, they shoot the bear, and then they bury it in a construction site."
—DAVID LETTERMAN

♦♦♦

"The state motto of New Hampshire is 'Live Free or Die,' which appears on license plates made by prisoners."
—JON STEWART

♦♦♦

"I can't wait to get back to New York City, where at least when I walk down the street, no one ever hesitates to tell me exactly what they think of me."
—ANI DIFRANCO

♦♦♦

"Las Vegas is the only place I know where money really talks—it says, 'goodbye.'"
—Frank Sinatra

On New York: "What else can you expect from a town that's shut off from the world by the ocean on one side and New Jersey on the other."
—O. HENRY

✦✦✦

"In Colorado yesterday, voters approved a tax on marijuana to fund the building of schools. In other words—kids, don't do drugs, but stay in the schools funded by them."
—CONAN O'BRIEN

✦✦✦

"It's not necessary to have relatives in Kansas City in order to be unhappy."
—GROUCHO MARX

✦✦✦

"The last time anybody made a list of the top 100 character attributes of New Yorkers, common sense snuck in at number 79."
—DOUGLAS ADAMS

Snarky States of America

Live free or die! Liberty and union now and forever! *Nil sin numine*! Into the future! *Dum spiro spero*!

Really?! These are real state mottos. And they fuckin' suck. They say nothing about their states except that someone at some point might have known a little Latin. Let's get real with some mottos anyone would be proud to see on a license plate.

∽

Alabama
A lot like
Mississippi—but
with football.

•••

Arizona
"But it's a dry heat."

Alaska
Masturbation capital
of the U.S.

•••

Arkansas
Like a third-
world country . . .
only closer.

California
Winning biblical plagues bingo

•••

Connecticut
Where turn signals are a sign of weakness.

•••

Delaware
First . . . and forgotten.

•••

Georgia
Without Atlanta, we're Alabama.

•••

Idaho
"Would ya like some fries with that potato?"

Colorado
Where you carry your $4,000 mountain bike atop a $750 car.

•••

Florida
Live your life so that if it were turned into a book, we would ban it.

•••

Hawaii
Get lei-ed!

•••

Illinois
Don't pronounce the "s," idiot.

Indiana
Come for the corn. Stay for the soybeans.

•••

Kansas
So flat you can watch your dog run away for a week.

•••

Louisiana
New Orleans! (And we're sorry about the rest.)

•••

Maryland
You don't need special shampoo for our crabs!

•••

Massachusetts
We don't tahk foony—you tahk foony. Ah you a cawp?

Iowa
Welcome to Iowa. We hope you brought something to do.

•••

Kentucky
Birthplace of the daddy uncle.

•••

Maine
Half hippie, half hillbilly.

•••

Michigan
Enjoy all four seasons . . . in 24 hours or less.

•••

Minnesota
Canada Lite

Mississippi
Litterasy ain't everthang.

+++

Missouri
Remember that time your flight
got rerouted? You were here!

+++

Nebraska
Football and corn. Sometimes
at the same time.

+++

New Hampshire
Fuck off.

+++

New Mexico
Red or green? That is the
question. The only question.

+++

Missouri
Remember that time your flight
got rerouted? You were here!

Montana
Birthplace of the letter bomb.

+++

Nevada
Want to win $1 million?
Bring $2 million.

+++

New Jersey
The Traffic Jam Capital
of the World

+++

New York
Yes, we are better
than you.

+++

North Carolina
Rushing to the bottom as
fast as we can.

North Dakota
North of South Dakota

✦✦✦

Oklahoma
Birthplace of the
Blizzafloodquakenado.

✦✦✦

Pennsylvania
Where playing the game
"Are We On the Road?"
Is Fun.

✦✦✦

South Carolina
Where the tea is sweet
and mac & cheese is a
vegetable.

✦✦✦

Tennessee
As seen on *Cops*.

Ohio
Things to do in Ohio:
1. Leave.

✦✦✦

Oregon
Wanna check out my new
electric car?

✦✦✦

Rhode Island
It's not the size that
matters; it's how you
use it.

✦✦✦

South Dakota
South of North Dakota

✦✦✦

Texas
We put the "'Murica"
in America.

Utah
Utah: 2,161,526 Mormons can't be wrong.

+++

Virginia
Where one can have an enter-lectual conversation

+++

West Virginia
One big, happy family . . . literally

+++

Wyoming
Nothing.

+++

Special Canada Edition:
Sorry.

Vermont
Where we have more miles on our snowblowers than our cars.

+++

Wisconsin
Where Americans go to make cheese . . . and fail.

+++

Washington
Noah called from the ark. He's picking us up in 10 minutes.

+++

Special Mexico Edition:
Spicy Canada

UNITED STATES CAPITOL.

Dear ... Americans

Straight from message boards, X (formerly known as ... who gives a shit), and comments sections, here are actual questions posed online by people not from 'Murica.

∽

"Why are Americans obsessed with the word 'literally?'"

✦✦✦

"Why are Americans are obsessed with happy hour and marinara sauce?"

✦✦✦

"Why do Americans call it tuna fish? Is there another species of tuna I'm not aware of?"

✦✦✦

"Why do Americans measure things in football fields?"

"It measures one foot? Whose foot?"

•••

"Why do you ask how I am doing and then not listen when I try to answer?"

•••

"Why do Americans love trucks? Like what are they putting in them?"

•••

"Why is GoFundMe an acceptable replacement for a health care system?"

"Do you even listen to the side effects at the end of those drug ads?"

•••

"Fahrenheit—can we be done with that nonsensical shit already?"

•••

"Why is there enough food on each plate at a restaurant to feed a small country?"

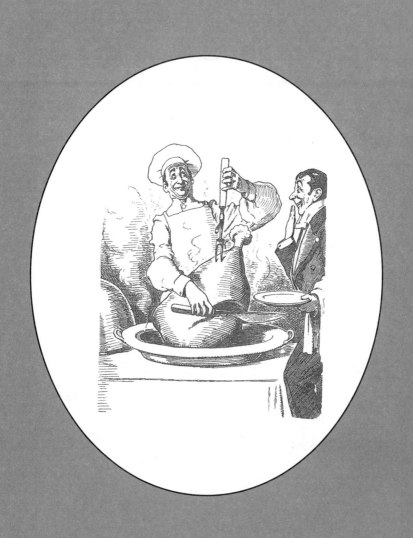

What's on the Menu Around the World

This quiz is for all you travelers who head to distant lands and bitch when you can't find a Starbucks. Live a little, why don't you!?

Haggis

Originating in Scotland, this tasty meal features minced sheep liver, heart, and lung, mixed with spices, oatmeal, and more. Oh yeah, and then all that is boiled in the sheep's stomach for hours. *Would you eat it?*

A. No.
B. Fuck, no.
C. Between starving and haggis, I choose starving.

Casu Marzu

Off the coast of Italy is the island of Sardinia. Casu marzu, means "rotten cheese" in Italian, and for good reason. Maggot larvae are placed in the cheese to help it ferment. The cheese should only be eaten while the maggots are still alive. *Would you eat it?*

A. Eating something that can jump up and get in my eye? No, thanks.

B. How do you say, "Get this the fuck away from my face" in Italian?

C. The words "food" and "larvae" should never be on the menu together.

Chapulines

In the Mexican cities of Oaxaca or Puebla, you will find these on street corners, and they are eaten like popcorn. But this snack food is decidedly not popcorn; it's cooked and seasoned grasshoppers. *Would you eat it?*

A. I would jump at the chance.
B. You're trying to sell me a bag of what?
C. With or without the antennae?

Balut

This delicacy from the Philippines, Cambodia, and Vietnam, is half-hatched duck eggs that are boiled or steamed and eaten from the shell. *Would you eat it?*

A. Eggs with legs? What's not to love?
B. I appreciate the offer, buy I'd rather eat my own eyeballs.
C. I'm sure there's someone out there a lot stupider than me who would enjoy this.

The Elvis Presley

This U.S. culinary collision of awfulness is a sandwich featuring bacon, butter, peanut butter, and a banana. And we're sure there are some versions that include sneaking in some mayonnaise. *Would you eat it?*

A. Always on my mind.
B. Return to sender.
C. Welcome to my world.

Kiviak

This dish from south-western Greenland, features five hundred small Arctic birds stuffed into a freshly disemboweled seal. The seal carcass is then sewn shut, buried, and left to ferment for months. To eat kiviak, you bite off the bird's head and then suck out the juices. You can also eat the whole bird with the bones. *Would you eat it?*

A. I'm going to sit this one out.
B. Offer declined.
C. I would, but my posse has advised me not to.

Are You an Obnoxious American Tourist Checklist?

Even if you don't do any of the things below, the only correct answer is still, "Of course you are!" Unless you are not from America. In that case, you have your own fucked-up things Americans think are obnoxious.

+ Do you wear American flag accessories or T-shirts?
+ Do you call people "darling" or "buddy?"
+ Are you wearing sneakers to everything and with anything?
+ How about white socks?
+ Are you telling your life story to complete strangers on a bus?
+ Fanny pack?
+ Sun visor or baseball cap?

+ Did you ask for a hamburger and fries at a local restaurant?
+ Did you ask for the ketchup?
+ Are you a little racist?
+ Are you confused when someone you meet doesn't speak English?
+ Do you then talk to them using the same words but slower and louder?

◆◆◆

"I suspect that LaGuardia is an elaborate prank, and New York has a real airport nearby that only locals know about."
—DAVE BARRY

"No matter how many times I visit NYC, I am always struck by the same thing—a yellow taxicab."
—Scott Adams

•••

If you're starting to look like your passport photo it's time to book a flight somewhere where you'll need your passport.

•••

Imagine falling in love with someone and then finding out they clap their hands when the plane lands.

"I have found out that there ain't no surer way to find out whether you like people or hate them than to travel with them."
—MARK TWAIN

♦♦♦

"No," says the guy from Kansas City. "Not if I have to explain it three times."
"I have found out that there ain't no surer way to find out whether you like people or hate them than to travel with them."
—MARK TWAIN

♦♦♦

Massachusetts news report: There's a driver driving the wrong way on I–80!
Massachusetts driver: One? I see at least fifty!

A man from Kansas City walks into a bar and asks, "Wanna hear a joke about people from St. Louis?" The bartender says, "Listen, pal, I'm from St. Louis, and I won't appreciate it. The man sitting next to you is 265 pounds, and he's from St. Louis too. And the bouncer, that huge guy there, is also from St. Louis. So do you still want to tell that joke?"

CHAPTER THREE:

That's

Entertainment?!

*M*ovies, books, TV, music, and more! We love amusing ourselves to the grave! And there's so much to watch, read, and listen to. It's all shit, but who cares! At least we don't have time to look into our souls for the meaning of life or anything like that. That would suck. Just sit back, relax, and consume this chapter as you would any other form of entertainment—with that glazed-over look of someone in the midst of a dopamine hangover.

"Television is more interesting than people. If it were not, we would have people standing in the corners of our rooms."
—ALAN CORENK

◆◆◆

"The Supreme Court says pornography is anything without artistic merit that causes sexual thoughts; that's their definition, essentially. No artistic merit, causes sexual thoughts. Hmm . . . sounds like . . . every commercial on television, doesn't it?"
—BILL HICKS

◆◆◆

"He has Van Gogh's ear for music."
—BILLY WILDER

"I love his work, but I couldn't warm up to him if I was cremated next to him."
—KEITH RICHARDS ON CHUCK BERRY

✦✦✦

"Television: a medium. So called because it is neither rare nor well done."
—DAVID LETTERMAN

✦✦✦

"I'd harbored hopes that the intelligence that once inhabited novels or films would ingest rock. I was wrong."
—LOU REED

If Your Life Were a Movie

Have you ever noticed that no matter what movie you're watching and what city it's supposed to be taking place in, every shithead gets a parking spot directly outside the building they are visiting? Even in fucking Manhattan! I guess the movie would run over if the hero or heroine had to park eleven blocks away, find enough quarters to feed the meter, and then hoof it to the diner to confront a potential bad guy; however, it would be nice if some of these things happened to us in real life.

+ Your arch villain will always helpfully tell you his or her plan instead of just killing you.
+ If someone runs into the room and tells you to turn on the news, the news item about you will always just be starting.
+ When you have a nightmare, you will always bolt straight up in bed, screaming.

- When you realize that she/he is the one, but they're on the way to the airport, you will risk life and limb racing to catch him/her before the plane leaves. You won't have to worry about security, and as you talk, everything will resolve. And no one will ever say, "Why didn't you just text me?"

- If you're a detective, you will only be able to solve a case after you've been suspended from duty.

- Caught up in a martial arts fight with a gang of thugs? Don't worry, they will wait patiently to attack you one by one.

- Knocked in the head by a falling brick, a gun butt, a baseball bat? Nothing to worry about because you will never end up with a concussion.

- However, one punch will knock your ass out whenever it's convenient.

- You will be able to pick any lock with a credit card or paperclip, unless it's the door to a burning building with a child trapped inside.

- No matter what you're shopping for, your grocery bag will contain one long baguette. But then the bag breaks, only round fruit will roll out of it.

- During all police investigations, it will be necessary to visit a strip club at least once.
- If you need to reload your gun, you will always have more ammunition—even if you haven't been carrying any before now.
- You will only have to reload your gun when it's time for some dialogue.
- Facial bruises and cuts will heal remarkably quickly.
- You will not bleed out like a stuck pig when you yank the IV out of your arm at the hospital.
- Instead of simply having a forty-five-second-long conversation with someone you're dating, you'll embark on a series increasingly bizarre hijinks until you both realize you're right for each other.
- Thankfully, every bomb you ever encounter will tell you exactly how much time you have left to diffuse it.
- When you are being chased, you will drop your keys before you can open the car door.
- Every hallway of locked doors will have one door that is not locked.

What They're Singin' ... What We're Thinkin'

Some song lyrics make you think of a lost love or pine for better days. Other lyrics are so shitty they make your eyes roll so far up into your head you can see your fucking brain. I mean, take LMFAO's "Sexy and I Know It." The lyrics include twenty-one instances of the word "wiggle." The song sold over 12 million units. That's 571,428 units per wiggle. These songwriters may be rich, but we're snarky AF—so there.

೧∿

"Well, I'd rather see you dead, little girl
Than to be with another man."

—The Beatles, "Run for Your Life"

Hey, Mr. War Is Over, you need help.

"Cause you were Romeo, I was a scarlet letter
And my daddy said, 'Stay away from Juliet.'"
                              —Taylor Swift, "Love Story"

So, we go from Shakespeare to Hawthorne and back to Shakespeare again? I get it. You were homeschooled, weren't you!?

+++

"Only time will tell if we stand the test of time."
                              —Van Halen, "Why Can't This Be Love"

Yeah, I don't have time for this shit.

+++

"Uno, dos, tres, catorce!"

                              —U2, "Vertigo"

Might want to check a Spanish to English dictionary, unless this is how they count in Ireland.

"I hate these blurred lines,
I know you want it,
I know you want it."

> —Alan Thicke, "Blurred Lines"

Hello 911, I'd like to report a crime.

+++

"England is my city."

> —Jake Paul ft. Team 10, "It's Everyday Bro"

And geography isn't your best subject.

+++

"I'm tryna find the words to describe
this girl without being disrespectful . . .
Damn girl, Damn, you's a sexy bitch."

> —David Guetta, "Sexy Bitch"

You tried. You failed.

"Clap along if you feel like
A room without a roof."

—Pharrell Williams, "Happy"

I get it! This is like "If You're Happy and You Know It" for old, sad people.

✦✦✦

"Monday, Tuesday, Wednesday and Thursday, Friday, Saturday, Saturday to Sunday."

—Black Eyed Peas, "I Got a Feeling"

Sesame Street called—Grover wants his song back.

✦✦✦

"On the floor of Tokyo, or down in London town to go, with the record selection and the mirror's reflection, I'm dancing with myself."

—Billy Idol, "Dancing with Myself"

Billy, doing a little self-idolizing, perhaps?

Movie Cliff Notes

Try this fun game: Use the fewest number of words possible to snark our favorite flicks. Here's a bunch we came up with, featuring snark galore!

∽

Titanic
Fuckin' sink already!

✦✦✦

West Side Story
Gang warfare . . . with snappy jazz hands.

✦✦✦

Chicago
No, Richard Gere cannot sing.

✦✦✦

Mamma Mia
The members of ABBA could probably act better than the actors of *Mamma Mia!* could sing.

Something's Gotta Give
Why does it feel like every Jack Nicholson smile should
be followed up by lawyers and an NDA?

+++

Dear Evan Hansen
A forty-year-old goes to high school.

+++

Fifty Shades of Gray
There's no climax.

+++

Mad Max: Fury Road
Let's go for a drive. Okay, now, let's drive back.

+++

A Man Called Otto
Grumpy Forrest Gump.

+++

The Shining
Airbnb gone wrong.

Cocaine Bear
Snakes on a Plane, but with a bear. And no plane.
With no Samuel L. Jackson.

◆◆◆

Any movie featuring Adam Sandler
Man-child learns a lesson, ends up with a woman
waaaaay out of his league.

◆◆◆

2001: A Space Odyssey
In space, no one can hear you yawn.

◆◆◆

Barbie
Down with the patriarchy! Up with Mattel stock prices!

◆◆◆

Oppenheimer
The History Channel without commercials.

◆◆◆

Beauty and the Beast
Stockholm Syndrome for kids.

Asteroid City
A how-terribly-clever Wes Anderson story within
a boring Wes Anderson meta story within a . . .
fuck it, I'm bored.

♦♦♦

Willy Wonka & the Chocolate Factory
Candy maker who uses slave labor slowly kills
annoying children.

♦♦♦

Tropic Thunder
"Look at us! We're inappropriate, but it's ironic,
so we can get away with it."

♦♦♦

When Harry Met Sally
Narcissistic personality disorder meets obsessive
compulsive disorder.

♦♦♦

A Christmas Story
A young boy picked on at school thinks a gun
will answer his problems.

Back to the Future
Boy goes to the past where fucked-up shit happens with his mom.

•••

Fight Club
Nobody talks about how stupid this movie is.

•••

Toy Story
A bunch of toys that can come to life traumatize a neighbor's kid.

•••

The Sound of Music
An ex-nun breaks up an impending marriage. Oh, yeah, and there are Nazis.

"Will you marry me? Did he leave you any money?
Answer the second question first."
—GROUCHO MARX AS RUFUS T. FIREFLY
IN *DUCK SOUP* (1933)

✦✦✦

"Oh, right, to call you stupid would be an insult to
stupid people. . . . I've worn dresses with higher IQs."
—JAMIE LEE CURTIS AS WANDA IN *A FISH
CALLED WANDA* (1988)

✦✦✦

"I make a habit out of doing things that people say
I can't do: Walk through fire, waterski blindfolded,
take up piano at a late age."
—JASON STATHAM AS RICK FORD IN *SPY* (2015)

✦✦✦

"If we get any more white people in here,
this is gonna be a suburb."
—QUEEN LATIFAH AS MOTORMOUTH MAYBELLE IN
HAIRSPRAY (2007)

Overthinking Superhero Movies

Because, you know what we all need? Another superhero movie.

∽

So where are all the other superheroes when it's not their movie? Sleeping it off?

✦✦✦

Wait, so Clark Kent managed to get an internship at a big newspaper despite being a high school dropout from Kansas?

✦✦✦

Whatever you do, don't become a father figure to Spiderman. You'll be dead before the end (or the beginning) of the movie.

Okay, so Superman has super strength, right? And he's totally ripped (Henry Cavill. am I right?!). But is there anything even heavy enough on Earth for Superman to work out with? Shouldn't he actually be flabby since there's nothing to do weight training with?

+++

How come whenever the Joker is in jail, no one ever thinks to take off his makeup to figure out who he is?

+++

Nothing quite like a superhero movie to get the crowd excited about billionaires.

+++

Nanotech: Any advanced technology that moves the plot forward, but which neither superheroes nor their script-writers understand.

+++

Iron, Man: Watch out for those unnecessary commas.

Mission accomplished: A superhero causing $3 billion in damage to a major city in order to save a cat in a tree.

+++

Didn't *The Incredibles* decide once and for all: no capes?

+++

Villain: Why is my villain calendar wrapped in aluminum? Superhero: I foiled your plans!

"About Superman and Batman: the former is how America views itself; the latter, darker character is how the rest of the world views America."
—MICHAEL CAINE

Snark: Made for Television

The following has been modified from its original version. It has been formatted to fit this screen. The small screen, in fact, is where most all the snarky writers go when they get fired from the movie set for being sarcastic to movie stars who will have you axed just for making eye contact. Here are some snarky quips from some of your favorite TV shows:

〜

Schitt's Creek
David Rose: You might want to rethink the nightgown first—there's a whole Ebenezer Scrooge thing happening . . . my best to Bob Cratchit.

✦✦✦

House M.D.
Dr. Gregory House: I'm sorry. I'm about to lose you because I'm about to drive into a tunnel in a canyon on an airplane while hanging up the phone.

Parks & Recreation
Donna: You guys will never believe what I just found on Jerry's Facebook.
April: A friend?

•••

Californication
Becca: Dad, do we look like the kind of girls who are into *American Idol*?
Hank: No, not so much. Actually you look like girls who would hurt girls who were into *American Idol*.

•••

Black-ish
Rainbow Johnson: If I'm not really Black, could someone please tell my hair and my ass?

•••

The Simpsons
Homer: Weaseling out of things is important to learn. It's what separates us from the animals . . . except the weasels.

Family Guy
Stewie: Hi. I'm Stewie Griffin. Tonight's *Family Guy* was a very special episode about drug use, but the simple fact is it's no laughing matter. To learn more about drugs, visit your local library. There's probably a guy behind there who sells drugs. Good night.

♦♦♦

The Office
Ryan Howard: Yeah, I'm not a temp anymore. I got Jim's old job. Which means at my ten-year high school reunion, it will not say 'Ryan Howard is a temp.' It will say, 'Ryan Howard is a junior sales associate at a mid-range paper supply firm.' That'll show 'em."

♦♦♦

Seinfeld
Elaine (to Jerry): Just when I think you're the shallowest man I've ever met, you somehow manage to drain a little more out of the pool.

Happy Endings

Max: If Mary Tyler Moore married and divorced Steven Tyler, then married and divorced Michael Moore, and got into a three-way lesbian marriage with Demi Moore and Mandy Moore, would she go by the name Mary Tyler Moore Tyler Moore Moore Moore?

+++

Modern Family

Sal: Sorry you couldn't come to the wedding. It was no kids.

Lily: It's okay. I'll go to your next one.

Cameron: She just means when she's not a kid anymore.

Lily: She knows what I mean.

"We have to be a role model for those little girls, because who do they have? All they have, literally, is the Kardashians. A whole family of women who take the faces they were born with as a light suggestion?"

—AMY SCHUMER

✦✦✦

"Television enables you to be entertained in your home by people you wouldn't have in your home."

—DAVID FROST

✦✦✦

"Imitation is the sincerest form of television."

—FRED ALLEN

✦✦✦

"When I started out in the 70s, there were three networks and 30 great comedy writers. Now we have 500 networks and 30 great comedy writers."

—JAMES BURROWS

All Stuck-up and Stupid Is No Way to Go Through Life

When Uncle Don or Cousin Lucy say stupid things at family get-togethers, we all laugh and make fun of them. And that's it! Luckily for us, celebrities have platforms very few in this world can even imagine, and they are so much fucking dumber than my Uncle Don and cousin Lucy.

～

"Listen, everyone is entitled to my opinion."
—MADONNA

♦♦♦

"I'm tired of pretending like I'm not bitchin', a total freakin' rock star from Mars."
–CHARLIE SHEEN

♦♦♦

"I'd rather smoke crack than eat cheese from a can."
—GWYNETH PALTROW

"Anne [Frank] was a great girl. Hopefully she would have been a Belieber."

—JUSTIN BIEBER

✦✦✦

"So, where's the Cannes Film Festival being held this year?"

—CHRISTINA AGUILERA

✦✦✦

"I guess I'm gonna fade Into Bolivian."

—MIKE TYSON

✦✦✦

"I've never really wanted to go to Japan. Simply because I don't like eating fish. And I know that's very popular out there in Africa."

—BRITNEY SPEARS

✦✦✦

"Get your fucking ass up and work. It seems like nobody wants to work these days."

—KIM KARDASHIAN

Reporter: "Did you visit the Parthenon during your trip to Greece?"
Shaquille O'Neal: "I can't really remember the names of the clubs we went to."

✦✦✦

"I'm my favorite rapper . . . my greatest pain in life is that I will never be able to see myself perform live."

—KANYE WEST

✦✦✦

"Humility and knowledge in poor clothes excel pride and ignorance in costly attire."

—WILLIAM PENN

✦✦✦

"You sure look real pretty in your glass house / You probably think you're too good to take the trash out."

—KACEY MUSGRAVES

What Shakespeare Really Meant*

Over the years, we have lost touch with Shakespeare language. Here is a helpful guide for you. "Who's Shakespeare," you may ask. Can't help you there, buddy.

༄

Self-love, my liege, is not so vile a sin, as self-neglecting.
Translation: We should masturbate more.

✦✦✦

Be to yourself as you would to your friend.
Translation: It's okay to sleep with your sister because your friend sure would.

✦✦✦

Have patience, and endure.
Translation: Use one of those numbing creams if you have to. Or try wearing five condoms at once.

That man that hath a tongue, I say, is no man, if with his tongue he cannot win a woman.

Translation: If you're desperate to impress her, you can always resort to oral sex.

✦✦✦

O, flatter me, for love delights in praises.

Translation: Honesty isn't necessarily the best policy when it comes to penis size.

✦✦✦

Praising what is lost, makes the remembrance dear.

Translation: When you're telling your buddies about your conquests, exaggerate. A lot.

✦✦✦

My endeavors have ever come too short of my desires.

Translation: You've never had twins and you never will. Get over it.

* Reprinted with permission from Scott Roeben.

You're Making My Ears Bleed

Snarky jokes about music and musicians? Sign me up!
There's nothing better than making fun people who
take themselves so fucking seriously. Like that dude
I met last week at a party. I mean, I know you're in a
band. I just watched you play "Roxanne" . . . poorly.

～

Classical music is like a vacuum. . . as soon as you turn it
off, it stops sucking.

✦✦✦

A night at the symphony: A musical experience that
starts at eight o'clock, but after three hours, your watch
says 8:20.

✦✦✦

Kid: Mom, when I grow up, I want to be a musician!
Mom: I'm sorry, dear, but you can't do both.

Q: What do you call one thousand screamo albums at the bottom of the ocean?

A: A good start.

Q: **What happens when you play country music backwards?**

A: **You get your truck, dog, and wife back.**

Q: What's the difference between a folk musician and a large pizza?

A: A large pizza can feed a family of four.

Q: **What's the difference between a pop star and God?**

A: **God doesn't think she's a pop star.**

Q: Did you hear about the guy who left his accordion in his car?

A: When he returned, a window was broken, and there were two accordions in the car.

Q: How do you keep your violin from being stolen?
A: Put it in a banjo case.

Q: What do you call a beautiful woman on a bass
player's arm?
A: A tattoo.

**Q: What did the heavy metal guitarist get on his IQ
test?**
A: Saliva.

Q: What's the difference between a banjo and an onion?
A: Nobody cries when you chop up a banjo.

Q: What do tuba players use for birth control?
A: Their personalities.

"I don't like country music . . . but I don't mean to denigrate those who do. And for the people who like country music, 'denigrate' means 'put down.'"
—BOB NEWHART

•••

Opera: When a guy gets stabbed in the back and, instead of bleeding, he sings.

What do you call a drummer in a suit?
The defendant.

•••

Taylor Swift at NFL Football Games: We love that you've gotten a whole new fan-base excited about football, but can you write a song about how the game is played for your fans?

Throwing Shade at the Movies

Movies are easy to critique, but it's so much more fun to throw snark at 'em. Ninety percent of these Hollywood ego trips are utter shit, and the other ten percent are Oscar bait featuring mopey actors in World War II dramas. What's not to hate?!

∽

Twilight
"I've had mosquito bites that were more passionate than this undead, unrequited, and altogether unfun pseudo-romantic riff on *Romeo and Juliet*."
—MARC SALOV, THE AUSTIN CHRONICLE

♦♦♦

Gotti
"I'd rather wake up next to a severed horse head than ever watch *Gotti* again."
—JOHNNY OLEKSINSKI, NEW YORK POST

Grown Ups

There's something reassuring about a bad movie that
doesn't ask you to think or feel or even pay attention . . .
we can all be happy D-minus students huddled together
in communal self-disgust in a D-minus world."
—STEPHEN HOLDEN, *THE NEW YORK TIMES*

✦✦✦

Freddie Gets Fingered

"This movie doesn't scrape the bottom of the barrel. This
movie isn't the bottom of the barrel. This movie isn't below
the bottom of the barrel. This movie doesn't deserve to be
mentioned in the same sentence with barrels."
—ROGER EBERT, *CHICAGO SUN-TIMES*

✦✦✦

Battlefield Earth

"*Battlefield Earth* saves its scariest moment for the end: a
virtual guarantee that there will be a sequel."
—DESSON HOWE, *THE WASHINGTON POST*

"*Valentine's Day* is being marketed as a Date Movie. I think it's more of a First-Date Movie. If your date likes it, do not date that person again. And if you like it, there may not be a second date."
—ROGER EBERT, *CHICAGO SUN-TIMES*

✦✦✦

50 Shades of Grey
"[The romantic leads] have the sexual chemistry of two unsalted saltines dunked in milk and smooshed together."
—ALLISON P. DAVIS, *THE CUT*

✦✦✦

"*The Snowman* is like if aliens studied humanity and tried to make their own movie in an attempt to communicate with us. This simulacrum contains all the requisite pieces of a movie, but humanity got lost in translation."
—BARBARA VANDENBURGH,
THE ARIZONA REPUBLIC.

The Village
"M. Night Shyamalan directs the material as if he'd written it (which he did), and not. Single friend dared tell him the truth."
—MICK LASALLE, *SF GATE*

◆◆◆

Fantastic Four
"My notebooks usually remains near my lap, but at this movie, it made involuntary trips over my mouth to cover all my gasping."
—WESLEY MORRIS, *GRANTLAND*

◆◆◆

"Nominated for Best Foreign Film, *Eat, Drink, Man, Woman*. Which is also how Arnold Schwarzenegger asked Maria Shriver out on their first date."
—DAVID LETTERMAN

"*Gravity* is the story of how George Clooney would rather float away into space and die than spend one more minute with a woman his own age."
—TINA FEY

✦✦✦

"Excited about all these up-and-coming leading men. (And their future on-screen wives, who could be born any day now!)"
—ANNA KENDRICK

✦✦✦

"Yes, I shot a few scenes out of focus. I wanted to win the foreign film award."
—BILLY WILDER

"An actor is a guy who, if you ain't talking about him, he ain't listening."
—MARLON BRANDO

...

"Stephen Spielberg is so powerful he had final cut at his own circumcision."
—ROBIN WILLIAMS

...

"A wide screen just makes a bad film twice as bad."
—SAMUEL GOLDWYN

Dear . . .

Here are some . . . let's call them director's notes . . . for some of our favorite entertainers, forms of entertainment, etc.

ᔕᔕ

Fast & Furious Franchise,

Here's a great idea for your next movie: Don't.

✦✦✦

Disney,

We have jokes, but we're not entirely sure our publisher isn't owned by you.

✦✦✦

Chris Evans, Pratt, Hemsworth, and Pine,

You're all lumped together because of your level of acting skill and indistinguishable facial features. But, in the debate over the best Chris, we have to go with Farley.

High School TV Show,

> You know that there are actual teenage actors avail-able, right? So, why does the sophomore protagonist look like he has his own teenage kids?

+++

Snoop Dogg & Martha Stewart,

> I love how your friendship has lasted longer than either of your careers!

+++

Cast of *Friends*,

> We recently read that when you didn't like a joke in the script, you performed them badly on purpose to force rewrites. How come the rewrites never happened?

CHAPTER FOUR:

Family, Friends, and Other Influencers

Most family trees have a bunch of nuts. Yeah, and other families have a bunch of fucking nuts. We would typically commiserate with our friends, but they're fucking nuts, too. These days, you can't get away from the crazy. On the other hand, without these people in our lives, we'd be stuck trolling TikTok influencers or seeing people we went to middle school with on Instagram who are doing way better than we are. So, love 'em or hate 'em, you're going to pick up your sorry ass and go to that family gathering. And the next time a friend calls, go out for that drink! You may regret it, but if you hole yourself up in your room all by yourself, your family and friends are going to think you're the one who's fucking nuts.

"There is no such thing as fun for the whole family."
—JERRY SEINFELD

+++

"Happiness is having a large, loving, caring, close-knit family in another city."
—GEORGE BURNS

+++

"Everybody knows how to raise children, except the people who have them."
—P. J. O'ROURKE

+++

"They should make broken family-style restaurants. They forget to come out and sing Happy Birthday. They're like, "We forgot, but we'll make it up to you next year."
—SAM MORRIL

"I have good kids. I'm trying to bring them up the right way, not spanking them. I find waving the gun around gets the same job done."

—Denis Leary

•••

"You wake up one day and say, 'I don't think I ever need to sleep or have sex again.' Congratulations, you're ready to have children."

—Ray Romano

They Fuck You Up, Your Mom and Dad

Talking to your parents can be like tiptoeing through a minefield. They wondered why you need a license to do just about anything in life, but now that they're over the hump and they didn't, you know, lose you or anything, they pretend like they knew what they were doing all along. We have created a few scenarios where parents and their adult kids try to converse. Choose which response most resembles your parents'.

1. Dad: Have you seen my keys?
Kid: They're where you left them.

Your dad would do which of the following:
    A. Laugh at your poor attempt at humor.
    B. Throw a shoe at you.
    C. Realize that his kid has a point and retrace his steps and find his keys where he left them.
    D. Tell you that you were adopted.

2. Kid: Mom, Dad . . . please sit down. There's something important I need to tell you.

Your parents' immediate response is:
   A. Mom: Oh, no you don't! You should just be glad your grand-parents aren't your parents. Then you'd have something real to complain about.
   B. Dad: When I was your age, I was thankful for what I had. And I had nothing. Look at everything we've done for you!
   C. Mom: Go clean your room. (Even if you're twenty-eight and own your own place.)
   D. Dad: Get a job! (Even if you're a VP at a brokerage firm.)

♦♦♦

3. Kid: I want you meet my new girlfriend/boyfriend/partner.

Your parents say:
   A. Mom: Very nice to meet you! Please take off your shoes, make yourself at home, and if you wouldn't mind filling out this questionnaire. . . .
   B. Dad: What does your dad do?
   C. Mom: So, I've been thinking about flower arrangements for the wedding...
   D. Dad: Call me anything you want—just don't call me late for dinner.

4. Kid: Mom? What's it like to have the greatest daughter in the whole wide world?

Her response:
- A. It's just such a blessing.
- B. I don't know, dear. Why don't you ask your grandmother?
- C. Why do you ask stupid questions all the time?
- D. Maybe if you'd respond to my friend request on Facebook you'd know.

♦♦♦

5: Kid: Got any good advice for me as I move into my own apartment?

Answer:
- A. Mom: Don't let the door hit you on the way out.
- B. Dad: Happiness is just a lack of information.
- C. Mom: Always wear clean underwear.
- D. Dad: I thought you moved out already.

♦♦♦

6: Kid: I'm quitting college, and before you say anything, Steve Jobs, Oprah Winfrey, Brad Pitt, Mark Zuckerberg, and Alicia Keys were all dropouts!

Their response:
- A. Dad: Yeah, but they're all either smart or talented. Or both.
- B. Mom: Well, I guess you'll find your way.
- C. Dad: Take some time to find yourself . . . a new place to live!
- D. Mom: That's not going to look good on your Bumble profile.

The Family That Snarks Together

Here's some snark featuring your favorite people: your fam. Just remember, you'll feel shitty later on if you start laughing. Because with family, You. Never. Stop. Feeling. The. Guilt.

"I just saw my grandmother, probably for the last time. She's not sick or anything, she just bores the hell out of me."

—A. WHITNEY BROWN

•••

"Parents get burned out in big families. You could even see it in the naming of children. It's always like the first kid, 'You were named after grandma.' The seventh kid: 'You were named after a sandwich I had.'"

—JIM GAFFIGAN

Dad Flu: An illness that causes the male of the species to be more helpless and sicker than any other family member. In moms, *the common cold.*

✦✦✦

"You know, Moe, my mom once said something that really stuck with me. She said, 'Homer, you're a big disappointment,' and God bless her soul, she was really onto something."
—HOMER SIMPSON

"My mother wasn't the protective type. When my father left, she told us kids, 'Don't think this just had to do with me. Your father left all of us.'"
—CAROLINE RHEA

✦✦✦

"[My parents] homeschooled me until I was sixteen years old because they didn't want me learning about sex or evolution, and as a fun fringe benefit of that, now I don't know about states either."
—JOEL KIM BOOSTER

An elderly woman decided to prepare her will and told her preacher she had two final requests. First, she wanted to be cremated, and second, she wanted her ashes scattered over the local tavern.

"Why?" Asked the preacher. "Then I'll be sure my husband visits me every day."

A father is a man who carries pictures where his money used to be.

—ANONYMOUS

An elderly couple was celebrating their fiftieth anniversary at a dinner party. The husband stood up and started telling the story of his dating habits in his youth. It seemed that every time he brought home a girl to meet his mother, his mother didn't like her. So, finally, he started searching until he found a girl who not only looked like his mother and acted like his mother, she even sounded like his mother. So he brought her home one night to have dinner . . . his father hated her.

(Text exchange)
Kid: Hey mom, where are you?
Mom: I'm on my way home from Target. Why?
Kid: You brought me with you.
Grandpa in church (whispering): Honey, I just let out a long, silent fart. What should I do?
Grandma: First, get new batteries for your hearing aids.

+++

(Text exchange)
Mom: Don't forget to finish your homework.
Mom: Did you take out the trash like I asked?
Mom: Did you feed the cat?
Mom: Dad and I decided to buy you a car.
Kid: OMG! That's awesome.
Mom: No. We're not serious. Just wanted to make sure you're getting my texts.

+++

Mom: Stephanie, do you think I'm a good mom?
Daughter: My name's Betty.

+++

Daughter: Daddy, why is it raining?
Dad: It's God crying.
Daughter: Why is God crying?
Dad: Probably because of something you did.

Dear ...

Mom,

> Thanks for turning off the electric mixer before letting me lick the beaters.

+++

Dad,

> I know you bought that Ferrari because your girlfriend thinks your hair is graying, but don't listen to her. She's only eighteen.

+++

Grandpa in Heaven,

> I want to die peacefully in my sleep, like you. Not yelling and screaming like the people in your car.

+++

Kids,

> Don't make the same mistake I did and remember this: You can take a vacation, or you can go on a trip with your kids, but they are two mutually exclusive arrangements.

Younger Siblings,

Don't be ashamed of who you are. That's our parents' job.

+++

Older Siblings,

My psychiatrist, upon hearing that you used to say I was adopted, has helped me find the strength to finally say, "AM NOT!"

+++

Dear Grandma,

You know the mashed potatoes you made the other day? I'm pretty sure you mashed up a bar of soap in there along with the taters. That's why we all got sick.

Mom to Family

Match the phrase in A to the one in B to come up with a proper Mom response. Even if she doesn't say any of these things, you know she's thinking them.

A. This is my cup of care . . .

B. I feel a spree coming on.

C. Yes, flowers say, "I'm sorry."

D. Someday you'll go far.

E. I think I'm emotionally constipated.

F. Oh, I didn't tell you?

G. Another chance?

H. There may be two sides to every story.

1. I haven't given a shit in days.
2. Sorry, I'm all out of chances. But I have this middle finger that has been on back order for you.
3. Oh, look, it's empty.
4. Cold, hard cash says, "I've learned my lesson."
5. Then it must not have been any of your fucking business.
6. But you're still wrong in both of them.
7. And I hope you stay there.
8. It's either a shopping one or a killing one. The choice is yours.

♦♦♦

Answers
A. 3; B. 8; C. 4; D. 7; E. 1; F. 5; G. 2; H. 6

Dad Jokes

Dads are subversive fuckers. They have created a world in which telling god-awful jokes is actually expected of them. It's like getting to fart in restaurants without restraint . . . wait, Dads do that as well. What the fuck?

∼

I used to hate facial hair, but then it grew on me.

✦✦✦

My first job was at an orange juice factory. Sadly I got canned . . . I couldn't concentrate.

✦✦✦

Whenever my wife is upset, I let her color in my tattoos. She just needs a shoulder to crayon.

✦✦✦

What's the most detail-oriented ocean?
The Pacific

I tell dad jokes but I'm not a parent. I'm a faux pa.

+++

What did the buffalo say to his son when he left for college?
Bison.

+++

If you can think of a better fish pun, let minnow.

+++

Did you hear about the kidnapping at school? It's okay now. She woke up.

+++

When does a joke become a dad joke?
When it becomes apparent.

Things All Dads Do
(fill in the blanks)

On the dark web there must be a site that only dads go to in order to learn how to do these things that all dads do. Every single one of these fuckers does all of these things. Maybe it's a disease, like a zombie apocalypse but only for people with beer bellies.

∽

A. Press the _____ four times.

B. Head to the airport _____ before the flight leaves.

C. Never letting you touch the _____.

D. Give you _____ instead of love.

E. Have a _____ phone case.

F. Love asking what _____ you took to get here.

G. Never admit to _____.

H. Always _____ when they sit down and then stand up.

I. Wear _____ sneakers.

J. Say _____ when you leave a door open on a hot day.

Answers:

A. Car lock button—elevator button and call buttons at traffic lights.

B. 10 hours—15 hours also acceptable.

C. Thermostat—remote control, toolbox, etc.

D. Money—he'll also fill up your tank when he borrows your car.

E. Wallet—that's if he's gotten rid of the belt loop one.

F. Roads—ostensibly so he can tell you a better way.

G. Being asleep—he was just resting his eyes.

H. Grunts—he may say, "Ah, that's more like it when he sits," and "Save my seat," when he gets up.

I. New Balance—Though Skechers are definitely catching on with the Dad set.

J. "Are you trying to air condition the whole neighborhood?"

Snarky Toasts

There's nothing quite like being the one who has to give the toast at a friend's wedding or at a big family anniversary. The worst part is that the people who want nothing to do with giving a toast are probably worth listening to. Anyone who wants to do it? They just like the sound of their own voice and will somehow make the celebration all about them.

～

To marriage . . . to some a small word, to others a long sentence.

•••

May all your ups and downs be between the sheets.

A wedding ring is like a tourniquet; it cuts off circulation.

Here's to staying positive and testing negative.

To our partners and lovers . . . may they never meet.

Always talk to your partner during sex . . . if there's a phone handy.

To friends . . . and the strength to put up with them.

May bad fortune follow you all the days of your life . . . and never catch up to you.

Without marriage, we would have to fight with total strangers.

To birthdays . . . not so bad considering the alternative.

To the bride and groom . . . So, I've prepared a brief PowerPoint presentation. Can you dim the lights, please?

To the three rings of marriage: the engagement ring, the wedding ring, and the suffering.

Greeting Cards from Snarkville

If you're under the age of ninety, you probably stopped sending out greeting cards the day they invented texting. But there are times when you care enough to send the very best. Other times, you send a note or something, but since you don't give a shit, it sucks. The following greeting card messages definitely show your lack of humanity.

To a snotty cousin's snotty kid:
I hear you graduated from kindergarten. Does that mean you stopped eating paste?

To an asshole teenager relation during the holidays:
There is no Santa Claus. You're sixteen, for god's sake.

To grandparents who have already written you out of their will:
In the immortal words of Pink Floyd, you're one step closer to death.

✦✦✦

To an older parent who broke a leg climbing a ladder:
You're too old to be this stupid.

✦✦✦

To a sibling:
I can't believe it's been a year since I didn't buy you anything for your birthday.

✦✦✦

To that friend who always wants to do karaoke:
I am intensely embarrassed to be your friend.

To anyone you pretend to love:
Always remember that you're someone's reason to smile because you're a joke. :)

✦✦✦

To a kid opening this card hoping for money:
Get a job, already. I mean, you're eleven, right?!

✦✦✦

A sympathy card for the annoying uncle who never stopped posting on Facebook:
I'm sorry for your loss. I'll miss those cute cat videos, too.

Top 10 Lies Parents Tell Their Children:

Why do parents lie to their kids? To protect them from some difficult truth? No! it's just to shut them the fuck up for five damn minutes.

1. Eat your vegetables and you'll grow up big and strong.
2. If you're not good, I'm calling Santa.
3. It's a grown-up haircut.
4. It tastes like chicken.
5. All the kids are wearing them.
6. Your teacher called and said you have to spend more time on your homework.
7. After a while, nobody will even notice your braces.
8. It's not about winning. It's about going out and having fun.
9. Someday you'll thank me.
10. This is going to hurt me more than it hurts you.

Top 10 Lies Children Tell Their Parents

Why do kids lie to their parents? Mostly so they don't get in trouble for something they were supposed to do but didn't or for something they broke. It's really just prep work for when they get jobs.

1. It wasn't me.
2. I'm not drunk.
3. I didn't steal it. I borrowed it.
4. I didn't take the car.
5. My homework's already done.
6. I've never had sex.
7. I forgot.
8. None of my friends have chores!
9. I'm not feeling well.
10. I ate all my vegetables.

The Family Bookcase

Ha ha, remember books? Looking at a family bookcase will tell you a lot about the people in that family. Leatherbound classics? Make sure they're actually books and not just decorative facades. Today's bestsellers? Have they ever been opened? And for our future—the kids—do they have any books Florida has banned? (It's a huge list.)

꩜

Books to Read to the Kiddos

Where the Wild Things Hide the Bodies
Oh, the Places You'll Scratch and Sniff
Don't Let the Pigeon Eat Daddy's Gummies
The Pocket Book of Items Confiscated by the TSA
Mommy's Stripper Pole & Other Things You Should Stop Licking
Charlotte's Web of Lies

If You Give a Mouse a Machete

Richard Scarry's Busy, Busy Pyramid Scheme

Frog and Toad are (Much More Than) Friends

Oh, the Animals You'll Meet on the Side of the Road Dead

You Are Different and That's Bad

The Boy Who Died From Eating All His Vegetables

Diseases Caused by Masturbation

Curious George and the High-Voltage Fence

Daddy's Trip to Rehab

Pop! Goes the Hamster . . . and Other Great Microwave Games

Shake That Baby: Fun with Your Little Siblings

Why Does Grandpa Smell Like Pee Pee?

Daddy Drinks Because You Cry

✦✦✦

Parenting Books

Last Child in the Woods: Outrunning a Bear

Secrets of the Baby Whisperer: Teaching Your Child to Say, "Huh, What's That Again?"

Our Babies, Ourselves: But Mostly, Ourselves
Confessions of a Slacker Mom: A Lesson in Three Pages
Fatherhood: On Twenty Minutes a Week
Siblings Without Rivalry: Keeping Separate Households in Different States
The Happiest Toddler on the Block: The Joys of Ritalin
The No-Cry Sleep Solution by Jack Daniels

"With kids, it's so funny because they're not strong enough to kill you. But they want to kill you so bad."

—TINA FEY

Insult Your Siblings Because You Hate Them

Siblings are like the kids *Lord of the Flies,* all fighting each other for whatever's left of their parents' love, affection, and attention. Here are a few top-notch things you can say to your dickwad sibs.

∽

You're the reason Mom's on medication.

✦✦✦

You look like a "before" picture.

✦✦✦

I'd slap you, but I don't want to make your face look any better.

You are more disappointing than an unsalted pretzel.

✦✦✦

I believed in evolution until I met you.

✦✦✦

You are the human version of period cramps.

Good story, but in what chapter do you shut the fuck up?

♦♦♦

I'm not insulting you; I'm describing you.

♦♦♦

I was hoping for a battle of wits, but you appear to be unarmed.

♦♦♦

Jealousy is a disease. Get well soon.

Don't hate me because I'm beautiful. Hate me because your boyfriend thinks so.

♦♦♦

Some babies are dropped on their heads. You were thrown against a wall.

♦♦♦

If your phone battery lasts all day, it's because no one likes you.

"The only thing that sucks about being a lesbian is that in order to have a baby that looks half like me and half like my wife, I need my brother's sperm. No straight girls ever need their brother's sperm."

—SABRINA JALEES

◆◆◆

I've reached that age where my brain goes from "You probably shouldn't say that" to "what the hell, let's see what happens."

Stupid Shit Old Fuckers Say

Some of you come from the if-you-quit-crying-I'll-buy-you-something generation. Old people came from the if-you-don't-quit-crying-I'll-give-you-something-to-cry-about generation. Be that as it may, here are some perfectly snappy, snarky replies to when old Aunt Susan starts bloviating at the next family gathering.

∽

I'm perfectly happy with my flip phone.
And I'm sure your computer still runs on Windows 98.

❖❖❖

Money doesn't grow on trees.
Come on downstairs with me; I want to show you my cannabis farm.

❖❖❖

The early bird gets the worm.
Yeah, but the late bird gets to sleep in and then get the late worm later.

Are you working hard or hardly working?

I'm hardly paying attention . . . to you.

+++

I ain't dead yet.

Well, you ain't so alive, either. Pick a lane.

+++

Youth is wasted on the young.

At least everything I say doesn't sound a little racist.

+++

Back in my day . . .

Back in your day, was time a construct yet?

Gray Pride: We're Tired; We're Old; Get Off Our Lawn

"Let me ask you a question: Why the hell do people keep getting married? Isn't anybody looking at the stats? I mean, one out of two marriages goes right down the shitter. If you were going skydiving, and they told you half the parachutes weren't gonna open, you'd be like, 'Yo, fuck that! I'm not going! I don't like those odds.'"

—BILL BURR

CHAPTER FIVE:

Holiday Fun

It's beginning to look a lot like "fuck this." It's the time of year for family, friends, and other cement heads to join together and annoy the shit out of each other. Good luck, everyone!

Celebratin' with Celebs! Whoa!!

Let's check in on our wise sages, the celebrities, the "oh wise ones," on what we should think about holidays, birthdays, etc.

"Halloween was confusing. All my life my parents said, 'Never take candy from strangers.' And then they dressed me up and said, 'Go beg for it.'"
—RITA RUDNER

"Thanksgiving is an emotional time. People travel thousands of miles to be with the people they see only once a year. And then discover that once a year is way too often."
—JOHNNY CARSON

"Hanukkah is the most American holiday because it's a celebration of burning oil that we don't have."
—ANDY BOROWITZ

"Thanksgiving, man . . . Not a good day to be my pants."
—Kevin James

"Nothing says holidays like a cheese log."
—Ellen DeGeneres

"Thanksgiving. It's like we didn't even try to come up with a tradition. The tradition is, we overeat. 'Hey, how about at Thanksgiving we just eat a lot?' 'But we do that every day!' 'Oh. What if we eat a lot with people that annoy the hell out of us?'"
—Jim Gaffigan

"Christmas: it's the only religious holiday that's also a federal holiday. That way, Christians can go to their services, and everyone else can sit at home and reflect on the true meaning of he separation of church and state."
—Samantha Bee

"It was on my fifth birthday that Papa put his hand on my shoulder and said, 'Remember, my son, if you ever need a helping hand, you'll find one at the end of your arm.'"
—SAM LEVENSON

The Four Santa Stages: 1. You believe in Santa Claus; 2. You no longer believe in Santa Claus; 3. You are Santa Claus; 4. You look like Santa Claus.

Hanukkah Books You'll Never See

Hurry, before bookstores run out!

❧

The Schmuck Who Stole Hanukkah: The story of a moron that tries to enter the village of Schvantzville to steal all the toys but can't seem to pick the "big" night.

•••

Good Night, Moon-orah: A very short book, it follows a child on each night as she says good night to her presents. Chapter 1: "Good Night, Dreidel." End of chapter. Chapter 2: "Good Night, Chocolate Gelt in a Mesh Bag." End of chapter. And so on.

•••

The Runaway Dreidel: A dreidel wants to run away because everyone thinks he's just a cheap little top with writing on it.

The Giving Tree (But Just a Little): A children's book that is instructional for parents, it tells the
story of a little Jewish boy who befriends a tree and is institutionalized for it.

+++

The Big Book of Maccabee Pop-ups: Oy, too many swords. You'll put your eye out.

+++

"Hey, Mom, thanks for the Hanukkah guilt."
"You mean *gelt*."
"Yes, that too."

+++

Gen X Hanukkah: My phone was at two percent, but lasted for eight TikTok videos!

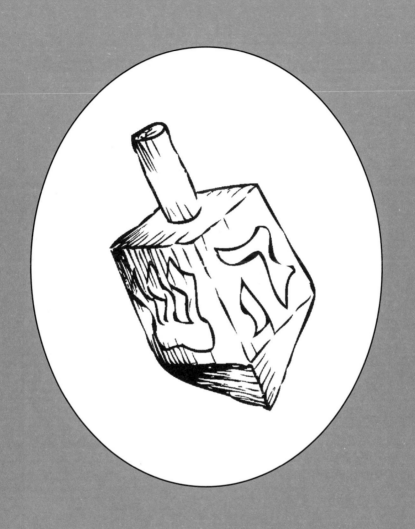

12 Days of Gifts

If you're looking for a gift-giving guide, do not come here. These gifts are for naughty nephews, nasty nieces, and other children you just wish would go away so you could watch football in peace.

1. Kenny the Kidney Stone Plush Toy
2. Fairly Serious Putty
3. The Lil' Electrical Outlet Licker
4. 5,200 Card Pickup: A card game that keeps the kids busy all day
5. Ginsu Boomerang
6. The Pee-wee Herman Pull Toy
7. Baby's First Spray Tan
8. Hasbro's Lil' Barber
9. Let's Duel!
10. Glitter Gun
11. Doggie Dentist Kit
12. Baking with Bacteria

Holiday Songs We'd Actually Love to Hear

No matter what holidays you celebrate, you have to admit that malls, superstores, grocery stores, etc. just do not give a shit. From Halloween till New Year's, it's Christmas songs for you. Here are a few we'd like to add to your holiday playlist.

∽

Jingle Hell
It's the theme song to this time of year.

✦✦✦

Have Yourself a Merry Acquittal Christmas
Grandma's getting out of jail in time for the holidays!

✦✦✦

Deck the Guy . . . Who Wrote This Ditty
Fa, la, la, la [BAM!] I mean, wouldn't you if you had the chance?

I'm Dreaming of a Withered Christmas
You know, updating a classic for climate change and all that.

+++

It's the Most Depressing Time of the Year
Let's all admit this and move on.

+++

[Your] Chestnuts Roasting on an Open Fire
Forgot what she wanted for Christmas, didn't you, you dope!?

+++

All I Want for Christmas
Is to stop hearing this fucking song.

+++

Last Christmas
If only.

Top 10 Responses to the Gift of a Holiday Sweater

You shake the wrapped box and by the muffled sound it makes you know it's another fucking sweater. This year, be prepared to act surprised and say something that will make gift givers wonder whether or not you're being snarky.

1. *Hey! Now there's a gift!*
2. *Well, well, well . . .*
3. *Boy, if I had not recently shot up four sizes, that would've fit.*
4. *This is perfect for wearing around the basement.*
5. *I hope this never catches fire! It is fire season, though. There are lots of unexplained fires.*
6. *If the dog buries it, I'll be furious! (Don't let on that you wouldn't be furious at all!)*
7. *I love it—but I fear the jealousy it will inspire.*
8. *Sadly, tomorrow I enter the Federal Witness Protection Program.*
9. *Damn . . . I got this the year I vowed to give all my gifts to charity.*
10. *I really don't deserve this.*

First Ten Years Anniversary Gifts

Nobody pays attention to this shit, but apparently, it's a thing. You get married, and for every anniversary, you get each other a gift made from something. What that means differs from person to person.

∽

1. Paper

What That Means To Her: Gift certificate for spa treatments

What That Means To Him: Paper for her printer

♦♦♦

2. Cotton

What That Means To Her: 410 Thread Count 100 Percent Egyptian cotton bedsheets

What That Means To Him: Lingerie

3. Leather

What That Means To Her: Henri Bendel Alligator satchel
What That Means To Him: A trip to the adult store near the highway exit

✦✦✦

4. Flowers

What That Means To Her: Bouquet of long-stemmed American Beauty roses
What That Means To Him: Flowers from Trader Joe's (Hey—there was a sale on beer!)

✦✦✦

5. Wood

What That Means To Her: Antique Cherry wood vanity
What That Means To Him: What happens when she wears year-two gift

✦✦✦

6. Candy

What That Means To Her: Belgium chocolate
What That Means To Him: Whitman Sampler

7. Wool

What That Means To Her: Cashmere

What That Means To Him: Hunting socks

+++

8. Linens

What That Means To Her: Lace tablecloth with matching napkins and table runner

What That Means To Him: Absolutely nothing

+++

9. Pottery

What That Means To Her: An antique Chinese tea set

What That Means To Him: A bong

+++

10. Aluminum

What that means to Her: Renting an Airstream trailer for that cross-country trip you've dreamed about.

What That Means to Him: Matching golf clubs

"I love Thanksgiving traditions: watching football, making pumpkin pie and saying the magic phrase that sends your aunt storming out of the dining room to sit in her car."

—STEPHEN COLBERT

CHAPTER SIX:

Generation Zzzz

*D*efined as people born in the late 1990s and early 2000s who "are seen as confident users of new technology." This generation is known for making friends online, using TikTok as a search engine, and spending six or more hours a day on their phones. (Not even pretending to be snarky here.) Overall, though, the worst thing about these damn kids is that they seem . . . what is it . . . oh, yeah, happy. Don't worry, all the other generations will ruin it for them.

"If you put an inspirational quote under your selfie, no one can see your narcissism."
—GANDHI

◆◆◆

"Everyone has a purpose in life. Perhaps yours is watching television."
—DAVID LETTERMAN

◆◆◆

"Life is pain. Anyone who says otherwise is selling something."
—WILLIAM GOLDMAN

◆◆◆

I was going to tell my friend a social security joke, but she probably won't get it.

Speaking Z

Match the Gen Z term with its meaning
(as best as we can decipher)

A. Suh
B. FamJam
C. Them kicks are drippin'
D. No cap
E. Weird flex but okay
F. Yee Yee or Slay
G. Yeet
H. I'm finna dipset
I. Fire
J. Mother (verb)
K. Say less!
L. Rizz

1. He or she is not lying.
2. I am in agreement.
3. Really cool.
4. Charisma
5. I understand.
6. Being iconic
7. Hello
8. Family
9. That's an interesting thing to say.
10. That's exciting information.
11. I'm going to leave now.
12. I like your shoes.

Answers
A. 7; B. 8; C. 12; D. 1. E. 9; F. 2; G. 10; H. 11; I. 3; J. 6;
K. 5; L. 4

Social Media Citation

Send one or all of these citations to all of your social media friends who annoy the shit out of you. That should be just about everyone. Except for you, of course—you would never do any of these awful things.

⁓

To: @_____
From: @_____

You have received this infraction for violating social media norms. It seems the rest of us know the proper protocol for posting and responding, but you haven't a fucking clue. I mean, you *know* we can see your posts, right?! Please stop doing the following immediately:

✦✦✦

Not switching out that shirtless profile photo
You're not going to score here; this isn't Tinder.

Liking your own status
This is some desperate, low-level shit here.

✦✦✦

Answering quizzes that steal your information
Actually, go ahead. We will ~~probably like~~ catfish you a lot better than the real you.

✦✦✦

Forcing us to read a long post and threatening to unfriend us if we don't read to the end / copy / paste / repost it in the next 24 hours
You realize this is how cults start, right?!

✦✦✦

Inviting everyone to everything
Nobody wants to go to your yard sale. Nobody!

✦✦✦

Self-congratulating
At least someone is happy for you.

Speaking to someone who is dead
We're pretty sure they don't have Facebook in heaven . . . but there's a special place in hell for people who do this all the time.

◆◆◆

Lurking
It's called "social" media, not "anti-social" media.

◆◆◆

Going over your inspirational quote limit for the month
The budget is 0–0 inspirational quotes allowed for you! And no, Albert Einstein didn't really say that. It wasn't Maya Angelou, either. Do some fucking research, and stop just copying and pasting everything you see between two quotation marks.

◆◆◆

Oversharing
The cringe factor of knowing how your colonoscopy went is off the charts.

Overposting
Give someone else a turn, for God's sake.

♦♦♦

Giving us cryptic status updates
We are waiting with bated breath to tell us what you are talking about! We are! Really! So go ahead and keep stringing us along, asshat.

♦♦♦

Posting anything about politics
Half of us have already hidden you after your last political outburst, and the other half just feel sorry for you.

♦♦♦

Giving out TV spoilers
There's a special place in hell for you.

♦♦♦

Selling something
Absolutely no one cares how long it takes that juicer to pulverize watermelon rinds.

Posting endless photos of your kids
We hate to say it, but your kids are just like all the other fucking kids on the internet. You realize that graduating third grade isn't that big a deal, right? I mean, we all do it sooner or later.

•••

Posting endless photos of your food
Wait, is that a fly in your soup?

•••

Posting gym selfies
We get it, you're fit. Well guess what? We are not, but we are happy.

•••

Posting how many attempts it took you to get Worldle
What's a five-letter word for asshole?

First World Problems through the Ages

It's time for a snarky history lesson. Let's take a look at what worried all the asshats from yesteryear to today.

∽

1934

My speakeasy is making too much money, and I don't know where to put it all.

✦✦✦

This dang Depression is making things really tough. Just the other day, I had to release three of my day maids.

✦✦✦

I can't afford all my mistresses!

1984

My hair won't stay up.

We can't get MTV where we live!

+++

All this cocaine is making it difficult to sleep.

2024

My childhood didn't suck, so I don't have enough pain to turn into art!

+++

My phone's almost dead . . . but my charger is over there (pointing to a location just out of reach).

+++

The restaurant's portion sizes are way too big.

"Mother Teresa didn't walk around complaining about her thighs—she had shit to do."
—SARAH SILVERMAN

•••

"Every generation is defined by a great struggle or tragedy. And it's wild that our kids will never know there was a period of time, in this country, where you had to make a choice between being online or being on the phone."
—HASAN MINHAJ

Signs You Might Be a Karen or a Chad Fill-in-the-Blank

According to Wikipedia, "Karen" is a pejorative term used as slang for a middle-class white woman who is perceived as entitled or demanding beyond the scope of what is normal. The term is often portrayed in memes depicting middle-class white women who 'use their white and class privilege to demand their own way.'"

Take this quiz to find out if you are one of 'em.

∽

1. If you've ever asked to speak to the _____.
2. If you take up two spaces with your _____.
3. If you've ever called the cops on a kid for _____ in your driveway.
4. If you live in a _____.
5. If you've ever followed up the statement, "I'm not a racist," with _____.

6. If you've ever complained about your _____ not being hot enough.

7. If you've traded in your SUV because it wasn't _____.

8. If you've ever left a 1-star _____ review.

9. If to you, the phrase, "my body, my choice," has nothing to do with _____.

10. You have an inverted _____ with sideswept bangs cut at an angle.

+++

Answers: 1. manager; 2. BMW; 3. riding their bike; 4. gated community; 5. "but."; 6. Pumpkin Spice Latte; 7. big enough; 8. Yelp; 9. abortion; 10. bob

> "In the wild, a group of Karens is called 'a complaint.'"
>
> —DEFINITELY NOT *NATIONAL GEOGRAPHIC*

Definitions of People We All Know

We like to categorize people. For example, outgoing people are extroverts, while introverts are people who wait for extroverts to ask them to a party. We, the authors, like to think of ourselves as snarkicists. That means we think we are better than everyone else, and to show our superiority, we snark the fuck out of everything. As all the mystics say: know thyself.

Askhole: A person who constantly asks for your advice, yet always does the opposite of what you tell them.

+++

Dobro: Hipster with money.

+++

Donald Ducker: Someone who walks around with only a shirt on.

Entremanure: Someone with a start-up business who knows nothing about anything and is just full of shit.

✦✦✦

Extraaaahvert: Partygoer who says hi to everyone and tries to hook everyone up. Please make them stop.

✦✦✦

A Gluten for Punishment: Person who isn't allergic to gluten but insists on gluten-free bread at the table, saying "I'm allergic."

✦✦✦

Hi-Bye Friend: A person you're not even Facebook friends with.

✦✦✦

Manifesterer: Someone who makes things happen, but those things are always rotten.

✦✦✦

Moana Lisa: Person who wants to complain but gets angry when you have valid solutions.

Momster: Parent who puts notes in your lunchbox. You're 27.

+++

Momster's Boy: See the second part of the previous definition.

+++

Monotonous: A person faithfully married to one person.

+++

Narcaholic: A person addicted to telling whenever you're breaking a rule, no matter how miniscule.

+++

Punchual: Someone so early for a party you want to punch them.

+++

Sasshole: Sassy but an asshole. Sarcastic wit keeps them from being a complete asshole.

Sexaphonist: A great sexter who blows at the real thing.

+++

Spatialist: A close talker.

+++

Stevia Daddy: He's not quite rich enough to be your sugar daddy.

+++

Villionaire: A rich person of dubious character and morals.

"When did avocado toast become the new crack cocaine?"

—WHITNEY CUMMINGS

Guess the TikTok Challenges

From licking airplane toilet seats to ingesting a mound of undiluted supplemental energy powder, TikTok challenges can be a lot of fun. But most of them just end up being fucking stupid and really dangerous. Yay, social media!
Here is a list of real TikTok challenges that have gone viral. Can you guess what they are and how many people were harmed?

1. #sleepychicken
2. #vampirefangs
3. #peeyourpantschallenge
4. #borgchallenge
5. #koolaidmanchallenge
6. #humanbowl
7. #cornchallenge
8. #benadrylchallenge
9. #poopchallenge
10. #milkcratechallenge

Answers:

1. Basting a chicken in NyQuil. *Truly a recipe for disaster.*
2. Supergluing costume vampire fangs to your teeth. *You know how superglue works, right? Right?*
3. Peeing your pants. *Not so much a challenge as a look into your future, eh?!*
4. Drinking a one-gallon jug of alcohol, electrolytes, caffeinated flavoring, and water. *Drunk, hyper, and hydrated—that's no way to go through life.*
5. Busting through fences like the commercials where the Kool-Aid Man bursts through walls and yells, "Oh Yeah." *You all know that hurts, right? And that the Kool-Aid Man isn't real?*
6. Pouring cereal and milk into a friend's open mouth as they are lying down, and then grabbing a spoon and eating the cereal. *So, where's the toast go?*
7. Sticking corn on the cob on a drill and eating it as it rotates. *Hello corn! Goodbye teeth!*
8. Taking a bunch of Benadryl so you will hallucinate. *This isn't even funny.*
9. Smearing your kids with chocolate or another melty item and telling them it's poop. *Forget college. Hope you're saving up for your children's future psychiatric needs.*
10. Climbing a pyramid of stacked milk crates without killing yourself. *It seems not everyone is succeeding.*

Newsflash! What the Fuck Happened Today?

Yeah, these are real headlines.

∽

Doctors Warn Against Using Erection Cream to Plump Lips
What's good for the tip isn't good for the lip!

♦♦♦

Man Destroys Wrong Beer At Walmart Amid Bud Light LGBTQIA+ Controversy
He knew the beer started with a "B."

♦♦♦

About Four-in-Ten U.S. Adults Believe Humanity Is Living in the End Times
And the other six believe it's already over.

Hipster Gets Mad His Photo Was Used in Article About How All Hipsters Look Alike, Then Finds Out It Wasn't Him
He also complained how not every hipster likes IPAs, while drinking an IPA.

♦♦♦

Gen Z Twitter Is Only Just Discovering What Meat Is Made of
Wait till they find out what's in their Jell-o.

♦♦♦

For Gen Z, TikTok Is the New Search Engine
This is a New York Times *headline, so if they have figured this out, Gen Z must have moved on years ago to something way cooler.*

♦♦♦

Tag, Kickball, Red Rover, Musical Chairs Deemed Inappropriate by Alabama School Board
They truly also banned yoga—hey, school board, how 'bout a nice game of lawn darts?

Dear ♦ ♦ ♦

Yeah, yeah, nobody writes letters or starts an email with "Dear." Go tell that to someone who fucking cares. Just read this and have fun for once, will you?

∽

Dear Apple,
  It's never "ducking." Never ever. And you're full of shot if you think it is. Go duck a duck.

♦♦♦

Dear X (formerly known as Twitter),
  Why does everything end up linking to OnlyFans?

♦♦♦

Dear Facebook,
  Can you help my great-grandmother remember her password?

Dear Instagram,

The idea of scrolling for interesting content assumes that at some point, there will be interesting content. Please advise.

♦♦♦

Dear Facebook User,

I'm sorry I didn't respond to your Messenger message. I was busy making my way in the 21st century.

♦♦♦

Dear Facebook Merchant,

Yes, I'll send you $200 for that thing you're selling. I'm sure it is exactly as described and that you'll really, really ship it. Do you take BitCoin?

♦♦♦

Dear Instagram Foodie,

No one gives a shit what you had for lunch.

Dear Healthy Influencer,

No one gives a shit about your diet. So shut up and eat your lettuce.

+++

Dear YouTube,

How come every time I start watching videos of cute cats I end up on some Neo Nazi page?

+++

Dear Facebook Troll,

Gosh, you're right! Your opinion, presented in ALL CAPS, is so much more valid than the previous post, written by a person with a PhD in the subject matter. Thanks for sharing.

+++

Dear TikTok Creator,

I'm only here for the tutorials.

Dear X (formerly known as Twitter) User,

Can you be more specific than, "I can't believe that happened!"? I mean, I literally cannot wait to read through the comments for that one person who figures it out and lets us know. Sorry I'm not hip enough for your vague post.

◆◆◆

Dear Child of Mine,

Thanks for letting me borrow your computer. You know they have Incognito Mode, right?! Can you at least erase your browsing history every now and then? Gross.

◆◆◆

Dear AI,

Write me a haiku that says, "That's okay AI, I didn't need my fucking job that much anyway."

Dear Content Creator,

I would have shared your meme, but I don't want to be associated with your horrific grammar, spelling, and punctuation.

Dear Person I Haven't Texted Back Yet,

I'm so sorry I haven't texted you back until now. I was trying to make up a good excuse and have finally given up.

•••

Rich Person Trying to Tell the Rest of Us How to Get Rich:

Life is 10 percent what happens to you, and 90 percent how much money you have. And from how much you've mentioned "Daddy" in two minutes, I'd say you've actually had very little to do getting that 90 percent.

Dude Saying Fuck the Doubters:
> Well, I hate to say it, but those you doubt you probably know you the best.

♦♦♦

Friend Bemoaning Yet Another Life Failure:
> You know, there's only one common factor in all your failures. You.

♦♦♦

Dear Person Trying So Hard to Stand Out So the Cool Person We're All Talking About Notices You:
> Yes, you're one in a million! Which means there are at least 8,000 people just like you. Probably more, actually. Yeah, definitely more.

♦♦♦

Dear Person Blaming the Haters for Not Liking His Ideas:
> Relax! You don't have haters. In fact, no one even knows who you are.

Demotivational Quotes About Life

Life is so damn short. And here you are reading inspirational quotes.

+++

Today will be . . . just like all the other days.

+++

When life knocks you down . . . stay there for a bit. Take a nap, even.

+++

Due to recent cutbacks, the light at the end of the tunnel has been turned off.

+++

Sometimes I feel sad to see everyone staring at their phones, but then I remember all these people could be talking to me. And that's worse.

There's someone out there for everyone. Well, except for you.

+++

Eat healthy! Stay Fit. Die anyway!

+++

By replacing your morning coffee with matcha tea, you can lose up to 75 percent of what little joy you have left in your life.

+++

If you never try anything new, you'll miss out on many of life's great disappointments.

"You tried your best and failed miserably. The lesson is, never try."
—HOMER SIMPSON

Things That Actually Suck

We all go around talking about things sucking all the time. The traffic this morning sucks. That new Netflix romcom sucks. Well, stop your complaining and read about these things that actually do suck. Big time. Proven by science. For real.

∽∾

Hippos: These mammoth asshole animals kill up to 3,000 people a year.

◆◆◆

Elon Musk: Realizing that billionaires are just lucky losers.

◆◆◆

George R. R. Martin: Finish the damn books already before I die. Hell, before *you* die.

◆◆◆

Websites: I've accepted all the fucking cookies already. Enough!

Concerts: $300 a ticket with scalper bots grabbing all the tickets up within 0.2 seconds of the site going live? No thanks.

+++

College: Pay $75,000 a year for four years so you can get a job making $40,000 a year.

+++

Tipping: Sure, I'll tip my waiter, my hairstylist, and my bartender, but everyone else? All you did was ring up a transaction.

+++

Repeating an Awesome Joke: Because no one heard it the first time. (Don't do it!)

+++

Taco Shells: Yeah, they're all broken. Or they'll break as soon as you put a piece of cheese in it.

+++

People who pronounce "vase" like "voz": You make me want to punch you in the foz.

"Better to remain silent and be thought a fool than to speak out and remove all doubt."

—ABRAHAM LINCOLN

✦✦✦

"If someone asks you why you're crying, you can just say, 'Because of how wrong you are.'"

—AMY POEHLER

I Don't Have Time For Your Bullshit

Here are some things you can say to asshat know-it-alls and other humans that are extremely difficult to misinterpret. (Try as they may.)

～

Hey train wreck! This isn't your station.

•••

Despite the look on my face, you continue to talk. Amazing.

•••

It's a great day to start leaving me the fuck alone.

Do not repeat yourself. I was ignoring you the first time.

•••

Are you always this much of an asshole, or are you making a special effort today?

I'd agree with you, but then we'd both be wrong.

•••

If you're waiting for me to give a shit, you'd better pack a lunch.

•••

"Don't be so humble—you are not that great."
—GOLDA MEIR

If it looks like I give a damn, please tell me. I don't want to give the wrong impression.

•••

"If your brains were dynamite, there wouldn't be enough to blow your hat off."
—Kurt Vonnegut

•••

"Every group needs its twat, and if you're in a group of people and there isn't a twat, then it's you."

—ANGUS WATSON

"It could be that your purpose in life is to serve as a warning to others."

—ASHLEIGH BRILLIANT

✦✦✦

"Life starts out with everyone clapping when you take a poo and goes downhill from there."

—SLOAN CROSLEY

CHAPTER SEVEN:

Weak Work . . .
I Mean,
Work Week

Yeah, we all have to work. Gotta make that living! But besides the five gallons of coffee we splash down our gullet every morning, what else is there to look forward to? It's simple: Might as well make the best of your dead-end job and be as snarky as possible. The only ones hurt by this attitude? Everyone around you. And who cares about them. If you like your job, you can happily skip this chapter and fuck off.

"People who think they know everything are a great annoyance to those of us who do."

—Isaac Asimov

When work feels overwhelming, remember that you're going to die.

—The Boss

Worker: Sorry I'm late. I broke down on the way here.
Boss: Did they tow your car?
Worker: Car?

Coworker: Everyone thinks you're really unapproachable and stand-offish.
Me: Really! That's the look I was going for!

The Boss

Until the end of all time, bosses will suck—up to the day you become one. Then, you know what? Bosses aren't so bad after all. And of course, you'll be a good boss, unlike every other boss you've ever had the pleasure of dealing with. Okay, let's be real: No, you won't. So, give up on your dreams of motivating your underlings with your commonsense approach to listening attentively, having empathy, and praising subordinates, and just give a few of these lines below a twirl. You'll be surprised how motivating you can actually be!

∾

I didn't say it was your fault. I said I was going to blame it on you.

✦✦✦

We passed over a lot of good people to get the ones we hired.

What you see as a glass ceiling, I see as a protective barrier.

•••

We're in the midst of a seismic synergistic paradigm shift. So, I'll have to get back to you later.

•••

How do you walk, talk, and perform rudimentary tasks without the benefit of a spine?

•••

To err is human, to blame somebody else shows good management skills.

•••

Some people climb the ladder of success. I, however, walked under it.

•••

My idea of a team effort is a lot of people doing whatever I say.

I would like to give you a raise, but (make something up).

+++

If I wanted your opinion . . . oh, wait a minute, that's never going to happen, so never mind.

+++

Ah . . . I see the fuck-up fairy has visited us again . . .

HR manager to job candidate: "I see you've had no computer training. Although that qualifies you for upper management, it means you're under-qualified for our entry-level positions."

"The brain is a wonderful organ; it starts working the moment you get up in the morning and does not stop until you get into the office."
—ROBERT FROST

Questions You Wish You Could Ask During an Interview

You made it past the résumé review (liar!), and HR wants to bring you in for an interview. If you really, really, really want the job, what are you doing reading this book? We're only here to bring you trouble. Anyway, see how these questions track.

1. What time of the month do you do drug testing?
2. Why did you hesitate when I asked you what you like about working here?
3. Can you speak lower, please? I have a hangover.
4. Since you're going to be my boss, why don't you tell me what *your* biggest weakness is?
5. Why can you be thirty minutes late to this interview, but I had to be here fifteen minutes early?

6. Can I have Fridays off? I have a date with with my couch.
7. I've got a call coming in. Do you mind if I take it?
8. What's the decorating budget for my desk?
9. How closely do you fact-check résumés?
10. It's okay that I listed my mom as a reference, right?

Bonus question: When you say open bar, do you mean "salad" or the other kind?

♦♦♦

Interviewer: The staring pay is $40,000 but later it can go up to $80,000. Interviewee: Okay, I'll start later then.

"Oh, you hate your job? Why didn't you say so? There's a support group for that. It's called everybody, and they meet at the bar."
—DREW CAREY

♦♦♦

"The reward for good work is more work."
—FRANCESCA ELISIA

Answers You Wish You Could Give During an Interview

On the flip-side of the interview process, there's this whole thing of asking "out-of-the-box" questions to interviewees. *If you were a pizza topping, what would you be and why? What's your take on garden gnomes?* Now close your eyes, and imagine yourself answering the following questions below the way we did. And then imagine yourself without a job.

∽

Q: What's your greatest strength?
A: I have an innate ability to answer stupid questions with a straight face. I can also whistle.

Q: **What made you leave your last job?**
A: **My boss told me to have a good day . . . so I went home.**

Q: Where do you see yourself in five years?

A: In line at the airport with a one-way ticket to Anywhere Else But Here.

Q: What's challenges do you expect to face in this role if you get the job?

A: Figuring out how long before I can call in a sick day. Or waiting the 90 fucking days until my vacation days kick in.

Q: **What makes you think you'll be a good fit for this position?**

A: **Oh, I think I'll be a horrible fit actually. My skills and expertise are no match for the paltry things you'll have me doing. But I need the dough.**

Q: What are your hobbies and interests?

A: Why? I won't have time for any of those things with this shitty job.

Q: Why do you want to work in customer service?
A: I'm good at pretending that I care.

Q: **Why did you apply for this job since it doesn't seem you have the experience?**
A: **How else am I going to get the fucking experience?**

Q: Why are diversity officers always women?
A: It's cheaper.

◆◆◆

Q: Why are coworkers like holiday lights?
A: They all hang out together, half of them don't work, and the other half aren't all that bright.

"It's true hard work never killed anybody, but I figure, why take the chance?"
—RONALD REAGAN

◆◆◆

"The trouble with the rat race is that even if you win, you're still a rat."
—LILY TOMLIN

Dear ✦ ✦ ✦

Your workday is long, and you don't have time to write to all the people who fucking piss you off. We've taken the pleasure of doing it for you.

∾

Dear Man Waiting for Elevator,
   I am entirely certain that pressing the "Up" button multiple times makes the elevator come faster.

✦✦✦

Dear Person Who I've Upset with an Insensitive Remark,
   Please tell me how I've upset you so I know how to do it again.

✦✦✦

Dear Person in Front of Me at Starbucks,
   If your coffee order is more than four words, you are part of the problem.

Dear Narcissist Co-worker,
  Feed your own ego. I'm busy.

***

Dear Person Accusing Me of Being a Jerk,
  I'll try being nicer if you try being smarter.

***

Dear Grammar Police,
  If your thinking I care about the difference between "you're" and "your," your wrong.

***

Dear Person Who Doesn't Appreciate My Snark,
  If you find me offensive, stop finding me.

***

Dear Know-It-All,
  Unless your name is Google, stop acting like you know everything.

Dear Person Who Took Credit for the Work I Did,
I hope your partner brings a date to your funeral.

✦✦✦

Dear Only Employee to Get a Promotion This Quarter,
Quitters never win, and winners never quit talking
about how they won. Please quit talking. Or quit.
Happy with either scenario. You know the universe
doesn't give a shit about you, right?

"Too many people spend money they haven't earned, to buy things they don't want, to impress people they don't like."
—WILL ROGERS

Sarcasm is the body's natural defense against stupidity.

Demotivational Quotes for Your Dreams and Aspirations

We all need something to cheer us up during an interminably long work day. Many turn to cheer-me-up posters, silly sayings on coffee mugs, and encourage sticky notes on your computer screen. None of these work for shit; however, replace "encouraging" with "snarky" and you may actually get through your day with a smile . . . along with a new evil, maniacal laugh.

∾

Never. Give up.

✦✦✦

Every morning, wake up and scream your dreams into a garbage can where they belong.

✦✦✦

There's no limit to what you can be if you lie to yourself.

The first step toward failure is trying.

+++

Dreams are like rainbows. Only idiots chase them.

+++

Not everything is a lesson. Sometimes you just suck.

+++

Reach for the stars! Follow your dreams! Live with your parents!

+++

Failure is always an option.

+++

Dream big. Then settle.

If you never believe in yourself, you'll never let yourself down.

+++

It's never too late to fail.

Every day is another chance to fuck it all up again.

+++

Try hard and don't worry if you fail because everyone expected that.

+++

Ironing boards are surfboards that gave up their dreams and got a boring job. You are an ironing board.

+++

Don't start believin.'

+++

There's too much blood in my caffeine system.

+++

Set low standards and consistently fail to achieve them.

+++

I Googled "Who gives a shit?," and my name wasn't in the search results.

It's a thankless job, but I've got a lot of karma to burn off.

♦♦♦

Meetings—None of us is as dumb as all of us.

♦♦♦

Work hard; complain harder.

♦♦♦

Crime doesn't pay . . . does that mean my job is a crime?

♦♦♦

Hard work pays off eventually, but laziness pays off now.

♦♦♦

Don't you just hate when you get to work and realize you forgot your will to live?

♦♦♦

Indecision is the key to flexibility.

♦♦♦

Hang in there, retirement is only fifty years away!

Aim Low, Reach Your Goals, Avoid Disappointment.

◆◆◆

None of your emails are finding me well.

"I love deadlines. I like the whooshing sound they make as they fly by."
—Douglas Adams

◆◆◆

"I always arrive late at the office, but I make up for it by leaving early."
—Charles Lamb

"Ambition is a poor excuse for not having sense enough to be lazy."
—Charlie McCarthy

◆◆◆

Supervisor: We've had four complaints from customers already this week. Do you know what this means?
Me: It's still Monday?

What I Said at the Meeting vs. What I Really Meant

Much of what we say at work is just a passive-aggressive suggestion that everyone else go fuck themselves. Refer to this list whenever you feel your passive-aggressive-ness veering toward plain, old aggressiveness.

∽

I'd like to hear other opinions.

What I meant: *Just agree with me and let's move on, it's almost time to go home.*

♦♦♦

I appreciate your feedback.

What I meant: *You know what will be fun? Stick your feedback up your very own ass.*

♦♦♦

I see.

What I meant: *I'm not listening to you.*

I will definitely look into that.

What I meant: *Not only will I not look into that, I was nodding so forcefully that I don't even remember what you just said to me.*

♦♦♦

Let's break for lunch and meet back in an hour.

What I meant: *I can't do this meeting on an empty stomach . . . or sober.*

♦♦♦

Seth has a PowerPoint presentation. Can you lower the lights?

What I meant: *I have a hangover, and the fluorescents are killing me.*

♦♦♦

Okay, thank you for your patience, and have a great weekend.

What I meant: *I saw you doze off, asshole. For that, have a mediocre weekend!*

I'm sorry this upsets you.

What I meant: *I didn't mean to push all your buttons. I was looking for mute.*

⁂

Please pay attention. This part is important.

What I meant: *You'd best not let your mind wander; it's way too small to be out there all on its own.*

⁂

Chaos, panic, and disorder—my work here is done.

I thought I wanted a career; turns out I just wanted the paychecks.

"I'm sick of following my dreams. I'm just going to ask them where they're going and hook up with them later."
—MITCH HEDBERG

Need a Day Off?

Fuck, yeah, you do. But try as you might, you can think of nothing your boss will believe to get you out of the office and back into bed. Only call with one of these following excuses if you already know the answer is going to be no, your boss is a bad listener, or you don't give a shit.

❧

I got on an airplane by mistake.

✦✦✦

The voices told me I'm needed at the beach today.

✦✦✦

I ate that piece of cake that was left in the breakroom a couple of weeks ago on a dare, and now I'm sick.

✦✦✦

I just woke up and I don't know whose bedroom I'm in.

✦✦✦

I feel homesick.

I finally watched the season finale of *The Bear,* and I'm too emotional to make it in.

+++

One of my 27 cats died . . . I think.

+++

I got all the way to work when I realized I was still in my pajamas.

+++

A neighbor just got caught cooking meth, and I can't get past the police barricades.

+++

I was trying the latest TikTok challenge last night, and I'm now at the emergency room.

+++

I'll be sick tomorrow. I'm telling you now, so I don't have to get up early tomorrow to do it.

+++

I just feel like my dog needs me today.

Fix the Résumé

If companies employ the use of fucking gobbledygook nonsense to try to explain why the third-quarter sales projections were so off, so should you when attempting to explain your less-than-stellar work experience up until this point. Here are some résumé-building "jobs." Can you guess what the real jobs are?

A. Beverage dissemination officer

B. Underwater ceramic technician

C. Personalized care associate

D. Director of first impressions

E. Vision clearance expert

F. Protein distribution engineer

G. Technology systems manager

H. Culinary artist

I. Entrepreneur

J. A service customer representative

Answers: A. Bartender; B. Dishwasher; C. Assistant; D. Receptionist; E. Window washer; F. Deli worker; G. IT guy; H. Subway employee; I. Unemployed; J. Exotic dancer (see what we did there?!)

The only thing worse than mornings are morning people. Oh look, it's fuck-this-shit o'clock.

•••

Out of the Office: I'll be back in 10 minutes. If I'm not back by then, read this note again.

I might look like I'm doing nothing, but at the cellular level, I'm really quite busy.

•••

I have plenty of talent and vision. I just don't care.

Spin Class

Finding a job after a run-in with the law can be an unpleasant experience. For one thing, updating the ol' résumé can get a little dicey. Here's our advice: Instead ignoring your past mistakes, lean into them! Show those headhunters that you have learned from your misdeeds by trying out some of the spin from folks who had some real problems.

～

1. "Woman Arrested for Live-Streaming Her Drunk Driving"
   I'm a young professional with a bright future who got thousands of hits on my latest viral video.

♦♦♦

2. "Prankster Cements Head in Microwave. Firefighters were 'seriously unimpressed.'"
   I'm a self-starter who's not afraid to ask for help when I'm stuck.

3. "A South Dakota man was arrested outside his home, which was on fire." (His company fired him not because he started the blaze, but because of his questionable decision-making abilities when he attempted to run into the house to save his beer.)
I can prioritize.

✦✦✦

4. Florida Man arrested after Waffle House Bacon Blowup
I expect greatness from myself and others.

✦✦✦

5. "Naked Lady Arrested Climbing into Her Ex's Chimney. The surprising thing is that it has happened before."
I am an outside-the-box thinker who is consistent with tremendous follow-through.

✦✦✦

6. "An Australian teenager was mauled after getting drunk and jumping into a crocodile-infested river to impress a woman he had just met. He denies being one of the stupidest people around."
I'm a tactile learner who loves adventure . . . and nature.

7. "Man Shoots Fireworks Off Own Head"
    Well, I'm dead.

    ◆◆◆

8. *Florida Man Arrested for Trying to Throw an
    Alligator on Roof of Cocktail Bar*
    *I believe in facing problems-head on and taking pro-
    active steps to stay on top of them.*

    ◆◆◆

9. Man in Contraption Washes Up in Florida After
    Trying to Run on Water
    *I believe there's nothing that can't be achieved if we work
    hard enough . . .*

    ◆◆◆

10. Florida Man Arrested After Trying to Cross
    Atlantic in Hamster Wheel Vessel
    . . . and I never give up!

Snarky Behavior at Work

You do realize that if Jim from the television show *The Office* worked with you that you'd hate his fucking guts. And what's not to hate!? He's disruptive, abusive, sleeps with co-workers, and behind that innocent grin lies a serial prankster who uses office time and money to terrorize. Nice guy. Here is some Jim-level shit you can do at the office without getting your ass fired. People will just look at you weird.

∽

When someone asks you to do something, ask if they want that supersized.

✦✦✦

To signal the end of a conversation, clamp your hands over your ears and grimace.

✦✦✦

Shout random numbers while someone is counting.

Carry your keyboard over to your colleague and ask if he wants to trade.

♦♦♦

Repeat the following conversation ten times to the same person: "Do you hear that?" "What?" "Never mind, it's gone now."

♦♦♦

Come to work in army fatigues and when asked why, say, "I can't talk about it."

♦♦♦

During the course of a meeting, slowly edge your chair toward the door.

♦♦♦

Arrange toy figures on the table to represent each meeting attendee, and move them according to the movements of their real-life counterparts.

♦♦♦

Put your garbage can on your desk and label it "in."

Reply to everything someone says with, "That's what you think."

♦♦♦

Finish all your sentences with "in accordance with the prophecy."

♦♦♦

Put mosquito netting around your cubicle.

♦♦♦

When someone asks why you are walking away mid-conversation, say, "You were boring me to death and my survival instincts kicked in."

"You know what a cubicle basically says? It basically says, like, 'You know what? We don't think you're smart enough for an office, but we don't want you to look at anybody."
—BILL BURR

Business Bullshit

People say things. All the time. Sometimes they know what they are talking about. If, however, they use any of the words or phrases below, you can rely on them being full of shit. Lots and lots of bullshit.

Core Competency: Fundamental strength, although one would think you'd want someone to shoot a tad higher than just "competent."

Buy-In: Agreement on a course of action. Can't just believe, gotta cost ya some jing to boot. Used to a much more useful effect in poker.

◆◆◆

Empower: Give added responsibilities to those below you.

Leverage: To manipulate or control. As in, to leverage your standing in the community to take unfair advantage over those lesser peons out there.

♦♦♦

Vertical: A specific area of expertise. Would really prefer it if you were horizontal, face on the ground.

Learnings: Bizarre conjugations now pass for "expertise." Go ahead and take the English Language and make it your own. No one will notice.

♦♦♦

Boil the Ocean: Waste time. If only you could, we could make the world's largest pot of moron soup.

♦♦♦

It Is What It Is: And the World Champion belt and undisputed King of The Obvious crown goes to . . .

10 Sure Signs You're Getting Fired

You followed the advice in this book, and now you're afraid you're going to get fired. That's your fault, not ours. Anyway, if you're not sure whether or not you've crossed the line and are about to get the boot, look for the following ten signs.

1. There's a cardboard box by your desk.
2. Your shift supervisor says they'll send you next week's schedule and that's the last you ever hear from them.
3. The boss comes in the office in the middle of their vacation.
4. Your company credit card isn't working.
5. There's somebody else at your desk.
6. You've been asked to train the new hire to do your job.
7. When the Karen complaining about you is the boss.
8. The folks in your carpool won't look you in the eyes.
9. You punch in on the computer, and the screen says, "employee not found."
10. You walk into work and your boss looks surprised to see you.

Sick Burns for the Workplace

These comments are best said under your breath while you're alone doing your thing. Say them just loud enough so the people around you know you're talking, but not loud enough so they hear what you're saying. When they ask you what you said, reply, "Oh, nothing." That'll drive everyone batshit crazy if you do it enough times.

᠊᠊᠊

Too many freaks, not enough circuses.

✦✦✦

How many people work here, you ask? About half of them.

✦✦✦

I see you've set aside this special time to humiliate yourself in public.

✦✦✦

It sounds like English, but I can't understand a word you're saying.

Too many people are saying that you're a nice person once I get to know you. Isn't that just another way of saying you're an asshole and I'll get used to it?

•••

I can see your point, but I still think you're full of shit.

•••

You are validating my inherent mistrust of strangers.

•••

Thank you. We're all refreshed and challenged by your unique point of view.

•••

Why stand out when you're born to blend in?

•••

Have a good weekend. Or don't. No one cares.

•••

The fact that no one understands you doesn't mean you're an artist.

I like you. You remind me of when I was young and stupid.

+++

I'm not being rude. You're just insignificant.

+++

I will always cherish the initial optimistic misconceptions I had about you.

+++

How about "never"? Is "never" good for you?

+++

I'm really easy to get along with once you people learn to worship me.

+++

I'll try being nicer if you'll try being smarter.

+++

If you find it hard to laugh at yourself, I would be happy to do it for you.

At an Office Holiday Party, Remember . . .

The words "office" and "party" should never, ever be used in the same sentence. If they are, don't believe it. "Office" is where work is done. "Party" is what you do after "office." So keep in mind the following advice the next time you are mandated to attend the next office party.

1. Nobody wants to sit on your lap.
2. You are not a stripper.
3. The boss's partner does not have the hots for you.
4. Don't say to your colleague's partner, "You're not as ugly as they said you were."
5. Nobody but you thinks you're the life of the party.
6. Photocopying your ass is so twentieth century.
7. You're not an action hero.
8. You're not the Kool-Aid Man (see page 211).
9. That co-worker you've had your eye on all year is not into you.
10. Never bogart the karaoke machine. Better yet, don't go near the karaoke machine.

Make That Bank, Bro

Actually, did you know that the best things in life are actually quite expensive?! Well, that's something we found out after we graduated with English degrees. Let's hear what all the fuckers out there who have made something of themselves have to say about it. Yes, please do enlighten us, oh wise ones!

"Money isn't the most important thing in life, but it's reasonably close to oxygen on the 'gotta have it' scale."
—Zig Ziglar

"Whoever said money can't buy happiness didn't know where to shop."
—Gertrude Stein

♦♦♦

"Always borrow money from a pessimist. He won't expect it back."
—Oscar Wilde

"Why is there so much month left at the end of the money?"
—John Barrymore

•••

"I'm tired of hearing about money, money, money, money, money. I just want to play the game, drink Pepsi, wear Reebok."
—Shaquille O'Neal

"They say money talks, but all mine ever says is 'good-bye' sucker."
—Jill Shalvis

•••

"If you want to know what God thinks of money, just look at the people he gave it to."
—Dorothy Parker

•••

"A bank is a place that will lend you money if you can prove that you don't need it."
—Bob Hope

"Cocaine is God's way of saying you're making too much money."

—ROBIN WILLIAMS

•••

"October. This is one of the peculiarly dangerous months to speculate in stocks in. The others are July, January, September, April, November, May, March, June, December, August and February."

—MARK TWAIN

CHAPTER EIGHT:

Snarky Sports

*H*ooray sports! Sport better than the other sporters are sporting! Do the things! Win the points!

Sports provide entertainment, exercise, heartbreak, and oh, so many annoying people. Sports also provide a microcosm of life in general. Some of the philosophical and poetic things we have learned from sports include a win is a win; you never score on the shots you don't take; the team that makes the most big plays wins, or the team that makes the fewest mistakes wins, or the team that scores the most points wins; it isn't over till it's over; height and strength matter; and life isn't fair.

Sportscaster Cliches

If you're new to sports, you may need a primer on what exactly a sportscaster is and what the actual fuck they mean when they use words. First off, there are usually two sportscasters assigned to a televised sporting event. One of them describes what is going on while you watch on the TV what is going on. The second one creates word salads of observations, statistics, reactions, predictions (that are almost always wrong), and most of all: clichés. Here are a few to check out if you're in the mood for smacking your forehead in disbelief.

∽

It all comes down to who wants it more.
How do you measure that exactly?

✦✦✦

Someone needs to make a play.
That's sorta why we're watching, isn't it?!

She's really giving 110 percent today.
Can't be done, Sparky. Might be time for that refresher math class . . . from the third grade.

+++

He's a hard worker.
He has no talent.

+++

He's silenced all the critics.
But you're still talking.

+++

They're just having fun out there.
Sure, they're up by 47 points.

+++

He understands his role on the team.
See: He's a hard worker.

+++

Anything can happen!
Anything except you shutting up for a damn minute.

You have to make your own luck.
Isn't that the definition of skill?

◆◆◆

You play to win.
Unless you're betting against your own team.

◆◆◆

Do you believe in miracles?
I'm not sure the dispenser of miracles is watching this (or any) sports game.

◆◆◆

This is the moment of truth.
So, were all the other moments lies?

◆◆◆

He's got ice in his veins.
The trainers should take care of that for him. Sounds dangerous.

◆◆◆

He got his bell rung.

He should be in the hospital—not on the field.

+++

She has the heart of a champion.
I hope she gives it back when she's done with it.

+++

It's a Cinderella story!
Who's the fairy godmother in this scenario—bibbidi bobbidi boo!

+++

It doesn't get any better than this!
Wanna bet?

"What's the difference between a three-week-old puppy and a sportswriter? In six weeks, the puppy stops whining."
—MIKE DITKA

Two enthusiastic fans were sitting at the Florida-Florida State football game on either side of an empty seat. "I wonder why anyone would buy a ticket and not show up for the game?" The Florida fan said. "Oh that was my wife's seat, but she died." The State man said. "Oh," said Florida fan, "I'm very sorry to hear that. But why didn't you give the ticket to a relative or friend?" The State fan replied, "Oh, I couldn't do that. They're all at the funeral."

•••

"How do you know if someone ran a marathon? Don't worry, they'll tell you."
—JIMMY FALLON

Match the Sex Euphemism
to the Sport

Match the sport to its euphemistic aphorism and giggle
like a kid from 1993.

∽∾

A. Soccer
B. Most sports
C. Football
D. Volleyball

E. Baseball
F. Basketball
G. Golf
H. Hockey

✦✦✦

1. Slipping it into the strike zone with a backdoor slider.
2. Putting from the rough.
3. Pulling the goalie.
4. Taking one for the team.
5. Taking it to the hole.
6. Stuffing in the end zone.
7. "It was Messi."
8. What a set!

Answers: *1. E, 2. G, 3. H, 4. B, 5. F, 6. C, 7. A, 8. D*

Golf! (If We Must.)

We want to dedicate this section of the book to all the golfers at the eighth hole on that course in our neighborhood. You know that honking that occurs when you swing? Yeah, that's us, driving by.

"I'm a golf fanatic," he said. "I think about golf constantly. I'll be out on the golf course every weekend, every holiday, and every chance I get. If it comes to a choice between your wishes and golf, golf will always win."

His new bride pondered this for a moment and said, "I thank you for your honesty. Now in the same spirit of honesty, I should tell you that I've hidden something about my own past that you should know. I'm a hooker!"

"No problem," said her husband, "Just widen your stance a little, and overlap your grip and that should clear it right up."

A husband and wife were golfing when suddenly the wife asked, "Honey, if I died would you get married again?"

The husband said, "No sweetie."

The woman said, "I'm sure you would."

So the man said, "Okay, I would."

Then the woman asked, "Would you let her sleep in our bed?"

And the man replied, "I guess so."

Then the wife asked, "Would you let her use my golf clubs?"

And the husband replied, "No, she's left-handed."

◆◆◆

Three guys go to a ski lodge, and there aren't enough rooms, so they have to share a bed. In the middle of the night, the guy on the right wakes up and says, "I had this wild, vivid dream of getting a hand job!" The guy on the left wakes up, and unbelievably, he's had the same dream, too. Then the guy in the middle wakes up and says, "That's funny, I dreamed I was skiing!"

"Why don't you play golf with Drew anymore?" Jeff asked Henry.

Henry replied, "Would you play with someone who moves his ball to a better lie when no one is looking, deliberately coughs through his opponent's backswing, and lies about his handicap?" "Well, no," said Jeff.

"Yeah, well neither will he."

♦♦♦

Tee: What golfers rest their balls on when they drive.

♦♦♦

"Although golf was originally restricted to wealthy, overweight Protestants, today it's open to anybody who owns hideous clothing."
—DAVE BARRY

♦♦♦

"There's a fine line between fishing and just standing on the shore like an idiot."
—STEVEN WRIGHT

Caddie Snark

We wonder if caddies like to screw with golfers as much as we like honking at them? Probably.

+++

Golfer: Any way I can cut ten strokes off my score?
Caddie: Yes, quit on the seventeenth hole.

+++

Golfer: I'd move Heaven and Earth to break one hundred on this course.
Caddie: Try Heaven, you've already moved most of the Earth.

+++

Golfer: Think I'm going to drown myself in the lake.
Caddie: Think you can keep your head down that long?

+++

Golfer: Son, how would you have played that last shot?
Caddie: Under an assumed name.

Four soccer fans were stuck on a deserted island when suddenly one of them died. In order to survive, the other three decided to eat the dead body. The first fan said, "I support Liverpool, so I'll eat his liver." The second fan said, I support Manchester, so I'll eat his chest." The third fan said, "I support Arsenal, and I'm not all that hungry."

✦✦✦

Newsflash! Authorities have just found the body of a politician in the Flushing River wearing a NY Mets jersey and bondage gear. They removed the Mets jersey to avoid any embarrassment.

✦✦✦

Joe Garagiola: "You amaze me Yogi (Berra), you've now become such a world figure that you drew more applause yesterday than either Prime Minister Nehru or Herbert Hoover."

Yogi Berra: "I'm a better hitter."

What a Comeback!

Having a tough time with some dickhead? Use the following out of context quotes from athletes to get 'em back. You will feel like a superstar afterwards. We promise.

To the person questioning your mental toughness:
"I'm so mean, I make medicine sick!"
—MUHAMMAD ALI

◆◆◆

To the person who is critical of your skills due to your gender:
"My coach said I run like a girl, and I said if he ran a little faster, he could too."
—MIA HAMM

When you want to practice humility in the face of
narcissistic assholery:
*"Nobody in football should be called a genius.
A genius is a guy like Norman Einstein."*
—FORMER QUARTERBACK JOE THEISMANN

♦♦♦

To that coworker who won't stop hitting on you:
"How much money do you have?"
—STEFFI GRAF AFTER A FAN ASKED, "STEFFI, WILL
YOU MARRY ME?"

♦♦♦

When a child you know or wants to drop out of school:
*"I quit school in the sixth grade because of pneumonia. Not
because I had it, but because I couldn't spell it."*
—ROCKY GRAZIANO

♦♦♦

To someone saying you're not doing a good enough job:
*"They say that nobody is perfect. Then they tell you practice
makes perfect. I wish they'd make up their minds."*
—WILT CHAMBERLAIN

To the game-night friends who think they're winning in Scrabble:

"So, who's coming in second?"

—LARRY BIRD

♦♦♦

When one of your kids is trying to get one over on you:

"I may be dumb, but I'm not stupid."

—TERRY BRADSHAW

♦♦♦

"We have a great bunch of outside shooters. Unfortunately, all our games are played indoors."

—COACH WELDON DREW

"We can't win at home. We can't win on the road. As general manager, I just can't figure out where else to play."

—PAT WILLIAMS

♦♦♦

"By the age of eighteen, the average American has witnessed 200,000 acts of violence on television, most of them occurring during Game 1 of the NHL playoff series."

—STEVE RUSHIN

Create Your Very Own Sports Movie

Here it is—a step-by-step guide to creating your very own sports movie. Most of the major sports already have several, so try handball or something. Don't worry, the formula works no matter how trivial the sport.

✦✦✦

1. Cut to the protagonist: a down-and-out coach with an awful car who struggles with the past: especially when he lost the big game when he was a player. Most likely the loss was due to something stupid he did.
2. Protagonist never went pro due to an injury.
3. The protagonist is given One. Last. Chance. As a coach.
4. However, coach doesn't get along with the star player, who is cocky until the coach starts working with him!

5. The star player was just misunderstood the whole time!

6. Coach doubts his own abilities and has dreams of screwing up all over again just like when he screwed up the big game . . . until a spouse, old friend, assistant coach, or plucky and incredibly precocious annoying kid comes along to help him believe.

7. Meanwhile, players have to overcome racism, sexism, poverty, or some other malady in order to play together like a team. And of course, nothing's been the same since the mill, mine, or factory closed.

8. The other team is bigger and better and cocky as fuck.

9. Someone has to die or get sick—preferably an assistant coach—for extra motivation for the big game.

10. Coach gives an emotional speech.

11. During the big game, the scrappy underdogs are down . . . but they have One. Last. Chance.

12. They make an incredible comeback on some sort of unlikely play, and they win. If it's an outdoor sport, it's probably raining.
13. Protagonist points to the person who believed in him in step 6 for a really long time.
14. Celebration in slow motion . . . fade out.

Q: What do you call forty people watching the Super Bowl?
A: The Detroit Lions

Q: Why do the Tennessee Volunteers eat cereal from the box?
A: They choke whenever they get near a bowl.

"The only reason I would take up jogging is so that I could hear heavy breathing again."
—ERMA BOMBECK

Looking for a New Sport?

This isn't really about staying fit or running off all the anger you've kept inside yourself all day. Instead, the definitions below are for sports you should watch on TV. We've helpfully "summarized" them so you know what to expect. "Trying" out a new sport is always worth a shot, and hopefully, you and your buddies will soon be watching semi-finals for darts on ESPN 18.

∽

Skiing: People in tight clothes catching colds and breaking bones.

✦✦✦

Golf: People slapping around dimpled balls all day. Khaki. Lots of Khaki.

✦✦✦

Basketball: Taking the fun out of catch for over 150 years.

Tennis: Lots of backhands, forehands, and grunting.

✦✦✦

Pickleball: Tennis . . . no . . . ping pong . . . played with a wiffle ball. Not sure if we're calling pickleballers athletes yet.

✦✦✦

Lacrosse: Hit 'em with your stick!

✦✦✦

Cycling: Competition to see who can withstand the most steroids.

✦✦✦

Rowing: Going nowhere, fast.

✦✦✦

Darts: Archery with a beer in your non-dominant hand.

✦✦✦

Cornhole: Not as dirty as it sounds.

Dear . . .

Sports are great, but that doesn't mean some things need to be addressed right now in this book. These "issues" have been bothering us for eons! So read up, and straighten yourself out already.

〰

Early Morning Joggers:

I see you inflicting unnecessary pain on yourself on purpose. I see that look of superiority, too. But I went for a run today, too . . . a donut run! And I'm into fitness, too . . . fitness last donut in my mouth!

♦♦♦

Pro Soccer Players:

The other day I was watching a game of Ouch! You almost touched me! when a soccer game broke out. Good work.

Dear Fans at Any Sporting Event:
You know you can fuck with your phone at home, right?
And it's cheaper.

+++

Basketball Players:
How do you find time to work out when you have all
those podcasts to do?

+++

MLB Baseball:
I know how to make the game even faster! Just play a
round of Rock-Paper-Scissors. Winner is best out of
three. Then we can all go home.

+++

Seven-Foot Basketball Player:
You playing basketball is like a fucking mermaid swimming the 1500m at the Olympics.

Dear Rugby:

I get the general gist of what you're doing, but it would be really helpful if you had the rules of the game running in a chyron—for the whole match.

✦✦✦

Dear ESPN:

Who you're going to fire next has become more interesting to watch than the sports you still have the rights to air. Oh wait, never mind. I see you've got the Cricket World Cup on at 2am tomorrow!

✦✦✦

Dear Sports Pundit Who Always Gets It Wrong:

You make a prediction, and then the opposite happens. How come you never say, "sorry"? What if we have a lot riding on this game and we listen to you? Can we sue? Have your lawyer call ours.

CHAPTER NINE:
Church
and
Snark

We here at Snarky AF wouldn't feel right not including a chapter on religion. There's a lot to be snarky about! However, we are not here to make fun of anyone' religious beliefs—just the people who practice these beliefs. This is because nobody is perfect, and where there is imperfection, just the right amount of snark can sneak in and poke fun at the lot of us.

The Snarky Separation of Church and State

Although He's regularly asked to do so, God does not take sides in politics. That doesn't mean smart people haven't noticed that politicians have no issues invoking the big guy whenever they need a few votes.

"If God had been a Liberal, we wouldn't have the Ten Commandments, we'd have the Ten Suggestions."
—MALCOM BRADBURY

"As a species we're fundamentally insane. Put more than two of us in a room, we pick sides and start dreaming up reasons to kill one another. Why do you think we invented politics and religion?"
—STEPHEN KING

"Those who say religion has nothing to do with politics do not know what religion is."
—MAHATMA GANDHI

"If God had meant for us to vote, he would have given us candidates."
—MARK TWAIN

"Sports, politics, and religion are the three passions of the badly educated."
—WILLIAM H. GASS

"Men play at God, but lacking God's experience they wind up as politicians."
—HARRY WILLIAM KING

"Prayer has no place in the public schools, just like facts have no place in organized religion."
—SUPERINTENDENT CHALMERS, *THE SIMPSONS*

"They always throw around this term the liberal elite. And I kept thinking to myself about the Christian right. What's more elite than believing that only you will go to heaven?"

—JON STEWART

♦♦♦

"I'm a born-again atheist."
—GORE VIDAL

♦♦♦

"I asked God for a bike, but I know God doesn't work that way. So I stole a bike and asked for forgiveness."

—EMO PHILIPS

Snark Doctrine

Taoism: Shit happens.

Buddhism: If shit happens, it isn't really shit.

Islam: If shit happens, it is the will of Allah.

Catholicism: Shit happens because you're bad.

Judaism: Why does this shit always happen to us?

Protestantism: Shit happens because you don't work hard enough.

T.V. Evangelism: Send more shit.

Hinduism: This shit has happened before.

Atheism: No shit.

Jehovah's Witness: Knock knock, shit happens.

Hedonism: There's nothing like a good shit happening.

Agnosticism: Maybe shit happens, maybe it doesn't.

Rastafarianism: Let's smoke this shit.

Existentialism: What is shit anyway?

Dear ◆ ◆ ◆

Rabbi,

> Why are you always going into bars with priests, ministers, imams, ducks, horses, and nuns?

◆◆◆

Pastor,

> I really liked your sermon today, especially when it was finished.

◆◆◆

Santa Claus,

> I get why people think you're a religious figure. You employ magic/miracles to get around; you have a beard, and you spend a lot of your time separating the good from the bad.

◆◆◆

Television Evangelist,

> It's hard to pray along with someone whose shoes are worth more than our house. Just saying.

God,

If you created the world, then you made snark. Sarcasm is your creation! So we're all good here, right? Right?!

+++

Atheist,

I get that you don't believe in God, but why do you think and talk so much about God?

Jews do not recognize Jesus as the Messiah, Protestants do not recognize the pope as the leader of the Christian church, and Baptists do not recognize each other in the liquor store or at Hooters.

+++

"Every day people are straying away from the church and going back to God."

—LENNY BRUCE

Divine Comedy

Q: Did you hear about the new low-fat religion?
A: I Can't Believe It's Not Buddha

Q: Why did god create man?
A: Because a vibrator can't take out the trash.

Q. What did the Buddhist say to the sandwich vendor at the ball game?
A. Make me one with everything!

Q: Why don't Buddhists have attachments?
A: Because they have no attachments!

Let me see if I have this straight: God wants me to let him save me from what he will do to me if I don't let him save me?

♦♦♦

I didn't believe in reincarnation the last time, either!

An atheist was rowing in Loch Ness, when suddenly the Loch Ness monster attacked him. The atheist panicked and shouted, "God help me!" Suddenly the monster went back underwater. A voice from the heavens said, "You say you don't believe in me, but now you are asking for my help?" The atheist looked up and said: "Well, ten seconds ago I didn't believe in the Loch Ness Monster either!"

◆◆◆

Biblical loophole: It's not premarital sex if you never get married.

◆◆◆

Two nuns ride their bikes down a lane. The first nun says, "I've never come this way before!" The second nun says, "Oh, it must be the cobblestone."

◆◆◆

"The only difference between a cult and a religion is the amount of real estate they own."

—Frank Zappa

Woman: God, how long is a million years to you?
God: A million years is like a minute.
Woman: How much is a million dollars to you?
God: A million dollars is like a penny.
Woman: God, will you give me a penny?
God: In a minute.

♦♦♦

Don't look back, the Devil might be gaining.
Doesn't really matter if you look back or not, he's pretty much got this race all sewn up.

♦♦♦

"I'm still an atheist, thank God."
—LUIS BUÑUEL

♦♦♦

"Pray, v. To ask that the laws of the universe
be annulled in behalf of a single petitioner
confessedly unworthy."
—AMBROSE BIERCE

CHAPTER TEN:

The State of Snark (Politics)

*P*olitics is such a hot topic of discussion amongst trolls and other monsters that it's getting harder and harder to out-snark 'em. They're getting smarter, wittier . . . hey, wait! Are they using AI? Anyway, here we go, stepping on toes, and pissing people off.

Republicans

It ain't easy bein' a Republican . . . Being a Republican means it's all right to be a bully. After all, God is on your side. Republicans are always right about everything: pro-religion, anti-bureaucracy, pro-military, and pro-business. It's their way or the highway (a highway built with American ingenuity, they would add). At the heart of it all? Money. The gathering and keeping of, hereto with . . . It's enough to make you want to . . . well, snark.

∾

"What is conservatism? Is it not the adherence to the old and tried against the new and untried?"
—ABRAHAM LINCOLN

"An honest politician is one who, when he is bought, will stay bought."
—SIMON CAMERON

✦✦✦

GOP: Greed, Oppression, Propaganda.

"Oh no! The dead have risen and they're voting Republican!"
—LISA SIMPSON, *THE SIMPSONS*

•••

If Republicans will stop telling lies about Democrats, we will stop telling the truth about them."
—ADLAI STEVENSON

•••

"The Republicans' health care plan consists of 'Just say no' to sickness.'"
—KEVIN POLLACK

Vote Republican. It's much easier than thinking.

•••

"A conservative is one who admires radicals centuries after they're dead."
—LEO ROSTEN

•••

"I'm not a Republican because I don't make enough money to be that big an asshole."
—PAULA POUNDSTONE

•••

How come Americans choose from just two people for president and fifty for Miss America?

Democrats

It ain't easy bein' a Democrat either . . . reaching out blindly, knowing what you want but not how to get it . . . that's a Democrat. Being a Democrat means you're only ever so slightly to the right of being a Liberal. You think the Bill of Rights might be "a little outdated." You smoked pot once, in college, and may have inhaled but "don't really remember, it was all a blur." You love NPR and PBS. You "really miss" the sixties, even if you were born ten years after they were over. The Party of Tolerance . . . as long as you agree with them. At the heart of it, Democrats are mostly just easy targets. Observe.

༄

"I am not a member of any organized
political party. I am a Democrat."
—WILL ROGERS

"If you get fifteen democrats in a room, you'll get twenty opinions."
—PATRICK LEAHY

◆◆◆

It was so cold this morning, I actually saw a Democrat with his hands in his own pockets!

◆◆◆

Democrats: Cleaning Up Republican Messes Since 1933

◆◆◆

Vote Democrat— it's easier than working!

The media are only as liberal as the conservative businesses that own them.

◆◆◆

"You have to have been a Republican to know how good it is to be a Democrat."
—JACKIE KENNEDY

◆◆◆

Democrats: The Party of Tolerance . . . as long as you agree with them.

"Sometimes I wonder whether the world is being run by smart people who are putting us on, or by imbeciles who really mean it."
—Mark Twain

"The typical socialist . . . a prim little man with a white-collar job, usually a secret teetotaler and often with vegetarian leanings."
—George Orwell

Why did God create Democrats? To make used car salesmen look good. Why did God create Republicans? To make used car salesmen look good. But you may ask, why then did God create car salesmen. Don't ask us, we're not fucking philosophers!

Dear ...

Political slogans are meant to rally politicians' supporters to get out and vote for their guy. However, every now and then, a slogan might inadvertently say less or more than it means. We've written some letters asking for clarification.

∼

Ronald Reagan,

You asked us, "Are you better off than you were four years ago?" If you were directing that to your millionaire buddies, then we think the answer was, "sure." Unfortunately "better off" hasn't trickled down to us yet.

•••

Richard Nixon,

"Nixon's the One" leaves a whole lot of room for interpretation. The one who what? Was the first to resign from office?

Barack Obama,

You said with such confidence, "Yes We Can!" But you didn't, did you?

✦✦✦

Jimmy Carter,

"Not Just Peanuts" had to be your slogan, even though you were a trained nuclear engineer?! However much respect we have for your accomplishments, you have to admit your administration wasn't just peanuts, but all sorts of other nuts, too!

✦✦✦

Bill Clinton,

"It's Time to Change America," you said. We think what you really meant was, "It's time to shortchange America."

✦✦✦

Lyndon B. Johnson,

"All the Way with LBJ?" You're not even hiding that you want to fuck us all.

Joe Biden,

You said, "Let's Finish the Job!" We're glad you're using a plural pronoun here.

+++

George W. Bush,

A safer world and a more hopeful America?" Thank you for your trustworthiness. As in when you once said, "I think if you say you're going to do something and don't do it, that's trustworthiness." Unless I misunderestimated you.

+++

Donald Trump,

Make America Great Again? Great at what? Sucking? Hiding classified documents in bathrooms? We could go on.

"I'll be long gone before some smart person ever figures out what happened inside this Oval Office."
—George W. Bush

♦♦♦

"The best argument against democracy is a five-minute conversation with the average voter."
—Winston Churchill

"I believe democracy is our greatest export. At least until China figures out a way to stamp it out of plastic for three cents a unit."
—Stephen Colbert

♦♦♦

"Democracy means simply the bludgeoning of the people by the people for the people."
—Oscar Wilde

Q: What is the difference between capitalism and socialism?

A: In a capitalist society, man exploits man, and in a socialist one, it's the other way around.

The Sick Burns of Barack Obama

During his eight-year stint as president, Barack Obama had some of the funniest jokes at the annual White House Correspondents' Dinners. So, Obama is either the funniest president ever, or his speechwriters are the funniest speechwriters ever. Hmm . . . wonder which it is . . .

"The White House Correspondents' Dinner is known as the prom of Washington D.C.—a term coined by political reporters who clearly never had the chance to go to an actual prom."

✦✦✦

"Dick Cheney was supposed to be here, but he is very busy working on his memoirs, tentatively titled, 'How to Shoot Friends and Interrogate People.'"

"He's warm, he's cuddly, loyal, enthusiastic; you just have to keep him in on a tight leash—every once in a while he goes charging off and gets himself into trouble. Enough about Joe Biden."

♦♦♦

"Now, I know that he's taken some flak lately, but no one is prouder to put this birth certificate matter to rest than The Donald. And that's because he can finally get back to focusing on the issues that matter, like, did we fake the moon landing? What really happened in Roswell? And where are Biggie and Tupac?"

♦♦♦

"Our chaperone for the evening is Jimmy Kimmel . . . Jimmy got his start years ago on *The Man Show*. In Washington, that's what we call a congressional hearing on contraception."

"I've made a few jokes over the years about John Boehner's unusual coloring. I used to think that it was a tan. But after seeing how often he tears up, I've come to realize: that's not a tan, that's rust."

◆◆◆

"All kidding aside, we all know about your credentials, and your breadth of experience. For example, on a recent episode of *Celebrity Apprentice*, at the steakhouse, the men's cooking team did not impress the judges from Omaha Steaks. And there was a lot of blame to go around, but you, Mr. Trump, recognized that the real problem was a lack of leadership. And so ultimately, you didn't blame Lil Jon or Meatloaf, you fired Gary Busey. These are the kinds of decisions that would keep me up at night. Well handled, sir! Well handled."

◆◆◆

"I'm taking my charm offensive on the road—a Texas barbecue with Ted Cruz, a Kentucky bluegrass concert with Rand Paul, and a book-burning with Michele Bachmann."

"And where is the National Public Radio table? You guys are still here? That's good. I couldn't remember where we landed on that. Now, I know you were a little tense when the GOP tried to cut your funding, but personally I was looking forward to new programming like 'No Things Considered' or 'Wait, Wait . . . Don't Fund Me.'"

•••

"I love the press. I even sat for an interview with Bill O'Reilly right before the Super Bowl. That was a change of pace. I don't often get a chance to be in a room with an ego that's bigger than mine."

"I used to say that politics was the second oldest profession, and I have come to know that it bears a gross similarity to the first."

—RONALD REAGAN

President Calvin Coolidge and his wife visited a government farm one day and were taken around on separate tours. Mrs. Coolidge, passing the chicken pens, inquired of the keeper whether the roosters copulated more than once a day.

"Yes," the man said. "Dozens of times."

"Tell that," Mrs. Coolidge replied, "to the president!"

Sometime later, the president, passing the same pens, was told about the roosters—and about his wife's remark.

"Same hen every time?" he asked.

"Oh no, a different one each time," the keeper replied.

"Tell that," Coolidge said with a sly nod, "to Mrs. Coolidge."

Fill-in-the-Blank Political Word Salads

Politicians have written speeches on teleprompters for a reason. And that reason is that, when left to their own devices, they can at times sound like a futuristic malfunctioning robot just before it blows up.

～

"Ukraine is a country in Europe. It exists next to another country called Russia. Russia is a bigger country. Russia is a powerful country. Russia decided to invade a smaller country called Ukraine. So basically, that's (1)_____."

—KAMALA HARRIS

♦♦♦

"We hold these things to be self-evident. All men and women created . . . you know, you know the (2)_____."

—JOE BIDEN

"(3)_____ has taken this year just since the outbreak, has taken more than one hundred years—look, here's the lives it's just it's just, I mean, think about it."

—DONALD TRUMP

✦✦✦

"Think of the people, if your kid wanted to find out whether or not there were—there's a man on the moon or whatever, you know, something, or, you know, whether those (4)_____ are here or not, you know, who are the people they talk to beyond the kids who love talking about it?"

—JOE BIDEN

✦✦✦

"The (5)_____ was an obscene period in our nation's history. I mean in this century's history. But we all lived in this century. I didn't live in this century."

—DAN QUAYLE

"Too many good docs are getting out of the business. Too many (6)_____ aren't able to practice their love with women all across this country."

—GEORGE W. BUSH

◆◆◆

"For seven and a half years I've worked alongside President Reagan. We've had triumphs. Made some mistakes. We've had some (7)_____ uh . . . setbacks."

—GEORGE H. W. BUSH

◆◆◆

"The internet is not something you just dump something on. It's not a truck. It's a series of (8)_____. And if you don't understand, those (8)_____ can be filled and if they are filled, when you put your message in, it gets in line and it's going to be delayed by anyone that puts into that (8a)_____ enormous amounts of material, enormous amounts of material."

—SENATE COMMERCE COMMITTEE CHAIRMAN TED STEVEN, EXPLAINING THE INTERNET

"But we have to pass the bill so that you can find out what is in it, away from the (9)_____ of the controversy."
—Nancy Pelosi

✦✦✦

"A zebra does not change its (10))_____."
—AL GORE

✦✦✦

"We (11))_____ there are known unknowns: there are things we (12) _____ we (13) _____. We also (14) _____ there are known unknowns: that is to say we (15) _____ there are things we (16) _____ we don't (17) _____. But there are also unknown unknowns—the ones we don't (18) _____ we don't (19) _____."
—DEFENSE SECRETARY DONALD RUMSFELD

Answers

1. Wrong; 2. Thing; 3. COVID; 4. Aliens; 5. Holocaust; 6. OB-GYNs; 7. Sex; 8. Tubes; 8a. Tube; 9. Fog; 10. Spots; 11–19. Know

---

"Things are more like they are now than they have ever been."
—GERALD FORD

✦✦✦

Several years ago, Reagan, Bush, and Clinton all went on a cruise together. While the ship was out in the sea, it hit an iceberg and started to sink. Quickly, Reagan yelled out, "Women and children first!" Bush then cried, "Screw the women!" To which, Clinton responded, "Do you think we have time?"

Match the Excuse to the Stupidity

Politicians lie the same way zombies eat brains—
methodically and often. Below are some real life lies.
Match them to what was really going on.

1. "The governor is hiking the Appalachian Trail."—a spokesman for South Carolina Governor Mark Sanford
2. "I actually did vote for the $87 billion, before I voted against it."—Senator John Kerry
3. "I was under medication."—Richard Nixon
4. "A number of things that I put in (the diary) were inaccurate, and some of them simply weren't true . . . On occasion, I discovered I would recount conversations that simply didn't happen."—Senator Bob Packwood
5. "Can I explain to you what happened? First of all, it happened during a period after she was in remission from cancer."—Senator John Edwards
6. "It may be tempting and more comfortable to just keep your head down, plod along, and appease those who demand: 'Sit down and shut up,' but that's the worthless, easy path; that's a quitter's way out."—Governor Sarah Palin

7. "[I have a] wide stance when going to the bathroom."—Senator Larry Craig
8. "I was hacked."—Congressman Anthony Weiner
9. "I was in a drunken stupor at the time."—Toronto Mayor Rob Ford
10. "It was just a tickle fight."—Congressman Eric Massa

Answers

1. This was regarding Sanford's week-long disappearance in June of 2009, when he was visiting his mistress in Argentina.; 2. Kerry' comment on voting against a military funding bill for U.S. troops in Iraq.; 3. What else?! The damn tapes.; 4. Packwood is referring to his diaries in which he boasted of his sexual encounters with staff members. 5. He was trying to explain his cheating on his wife while she had cancer. 6. She was explaining why she was quitting her job as governor. 7. Explaining his behavior after being arrested in an airport restroom for soliciting sex by playing footsie with an undercover officer in the next stall. 8. How a picture of his "bulge" ended up being sexted to a young woman using the social media handle "Carlos Danger." 9. Explaining how he came to use crack cocaine. 10. Explaining away complaints that he sexually harassed a male staffer. He explained it to Glenn Beck: "Not only did I grope, I tickled him until he couldn't breathe."

"Politics Is . . ."

". . . the art of looking for trouble, finding it whether it exists or not, diagnosing it incorrectly, and applying the wrong remedy."
—GROUCHO MARX

•••

". . . made up largely of irrelevancies."
—DALTON CAMP

". . . perhaps the only profession for which no preparation is thought necessary."
—ROBERT LOUIS STEVENSON

•••

". . . the art of postponing decisions until they are no longer relevant."
—HENRI QUEUILLE

"... the skilled use of blunt objects."
—LESTER B. PEARSON

♦♦♦

"... is like football; if you see daylight, go through the hole."
—JOHN F. KENNEDY

"... the art of preventing people from sticking their noses in things that are properly their business."
—PAUL VALERY

"Democracy means government by discussion, but it is only effective if you can stop people talking."
—CLEMENT ATLEE

"Democracy is a process by which the people are free to choose the man who will get all the blame."
—LAURENCE J. PETER

Oval Office Admissions

Politicians say the darndest things. Asshats, all of them.

✌

"If I don't have a woman for three days, I get terrible headaches."
—JOHN F. KENNEDY

•••

"You don't know how to lie. If you can't lie, you'll never go anywhere."
—RICHARD NIXON

"When they call the roll in the Senate, the senators do not know whether to answer 'present' or 'not guilty.'"
—THEODORE ROOSEVELT

"I am not fit for this office and should never have been here."
—WARREN G. HARDING

•••

"No man who ever held the office of president would congratulate a friend on obtaining it."
—JOHN ADAMS

•••

"If you want a friend in Washington, get a dog."
—HARRY S. TRUMAN

"Blessed are the young, for they will inherit the national debt."

—HERBERT HOOVER

◆◆◆

"Secret. This is secret information. Look. Look at this. This was done by the military and given to me."

—DONALD TRUMP

◆◆◆

"If one morning I walked on top of the water across the Potomac River, the headline that afternoon would read: 'President Can't Swim.'"

—LYNDON B. JOHNSON

"He's got his headquarters where his hindquarters ought to be."

—ABRAHAM LINCOLN

◆◆◆

"He can compress the most words into the smallest ideas of any man I ever met."

—ABRAHAM LINCOLN

◆◆◆

"No use for their heads except to serve as a knot to keep their bodies from unraveling."

—WOODROW WILSON

"I have left orders to be awakened at any time in case there is a national emergency—even if I'm in a cabinet meeting."
—RONALD REAGAN

•••

"Despite many obstacles, much has changed during my time in office. Four years ago, I was locked in a brutal primary battle with Hillary Clinton. Four years later, she won't stop drunk-texting me from Cartagena."
—BARACK OBAMA

"Sorry losers and haters, but my I.Q. is one of the highest—and you all know it! Please don't feel so stupid or insecure. It's not your fault."
—DONALD TRUMP

•••

'My esteem in this country has gone up substantially. It is very nice now when people wave at me, they use all their fingers."
—JIMMY CARTER

"If this is coffee, please bring me some tea; but if this is tea, please bring me some coffee."
—ABRAHAM LINCOLN

✦✦✦

"There is nothing left to do but get drunk."
—FRANKLIN PIERCE, (ALLEGEDLY) RESPONDING TO WHAT HE PLANNED TO DO AFTER LEAVING OFFICE.

"I don't know whether it's the finest public housing in America or the crown jewel of the American penal system."
—BILL CLINTON, SPEAKING ABOUT THE WHITE HOUSE.

On his deathbed, a lifelong Republican announced he was switching to the Democrats. "Why are you doing this," a friend asked. The sick man replied, "I'd rather it was one of them that dies."

President on President

U.S. presidents always pretend to hold each other in high regard. If you think they all actually liked each other, however, you're high. Match the president with his description by another president.

A. Gerald Ford
B. Barack Obama
C. Donald Trump
D. Jimmy Carter
E. Bill Clinton

♦♦♦

1. He's a "bozo."
2. If we were in high school, I'd take him behind the gym and beat the hell out of him.
3. On hearing he was going to be on the news show *60 Minutes*: "But that would leave 59 minutes to fill."

4. He's a nice guy, but he played too much football with his helmet off.

5. When he became president, he didn't know anything. This guy didn't know a thing. And honestly, today he knows less.

•••

Answers: A. 4 (said by Lyndon Johnson); B. 5 (said by Donald Trump); C. 2 (said by Joe Biden); D. 3 (said by Ronald Reagan); E. 1 (said by George H. W. Bush)

"Democracy substitutes election by the incompetent many for appointment by the corrupt few."
—GEORGE BERNARD SHAW

•••

"One way to make sure crime doesn't pay would be to let the government run it."
—RONALD REAGAN

Presidential Firsts

This huge quiz is the greatest quiz ever. The best quiz. You'll never get it because no one is as smart as me. And you're rude and stupid and scary, and I'm not attracted to you, either. Anyway, name the president who accomplished these "firsts."

1. First president indicted by a grand jury in a federal case.
2. First president indicted by a grand jury in a state case.
3. First president impeached twice by Congress.
4. First president to ever have an arrest warrant issued against him by a foreign nation.
5. First president to fail to ensure a peaceful transfer of power.
6. First president to never hit at 50 percent approval rating at any point during their presidency.
7. First president to have children from three different wives.
8. First president to assume office without having had any prior public service experience.
9. First president to be indicted by a grand jury in a federal case for actions taken while in office.
10. First president to be the subject of a mug shot.

Answers: 1–10: Donald Trump

Government, Can't Live with It, Can't Live with It: Demotivational Quotes

Wise words about an institution don't attract wise people.

∽

"When it comes to facing up to serious problems, each candidate will pledge to appoint a committee. And what is a committee? A group of the unwilling, picked from the unfit, to do the unnecessary. But it all sounds great in a campaign speech."
—RICHARD LONG HARKNESS

♦♦♦

"I honestly believe there are people so excited over this election that they must think that the president has something to do with running this country."
—WILL ROGERS

"Giving money and power to government is like giving whiskey and car keys to teenage boys."
—P. J. O'Rourke

"As usual, the Liberals offer a mixture of sound and original ideas. Unfortunately none of the sound ideas are original and none of the original ideas are sound."
—Harold MacMillan

"Conservative, n: A statesman who is enamored of existing evils, as distinguished from the Liberal who wishes to replace them with others."
—Ambrose Bierce

"A conservative is a man with two perfectly good legs who, however, has never learned how to walk forward."
—Franklin D. Roosevelt

Bart Simpson: "Didn't you wonder why you were getting checks for doing absolutely nothing?"

Grampa Simpson: "I figured because the Democrats were in power again."

✦✦✦

"The government is like a baby's alimentary canal, with a happy appetite at one end and no responsibility at the other."
—RONALD REAGAN

✦✦✦

"If presidents don't do it to their wives, they do it the country."
—MEL BROOKS

✦✦✦

"Nixon told us he was going to take crime out of the streets. He did. He took it into the damn White House."
—RALPH ABERNATHY

"There is no kind of dishonesty into which otherwise good people more easily and frequently fall than that of defrauding the government."
—BENJAMIN FRANKLIN

•••

"When they call the roll in the Senate, the Senators do not know whether to answer 'present' or 'not guilty.'"
—TEDDY ROOSEVELT

•••

"Asking an incumbent member of Congress to vote for term limits is a bit like asking a chicken to vote for Colonel Sanders."
—BOB INGLIS

"Government is the entertainment division of the military-industrial complex."
—FRANK ZAPPA

✦✦✦

"Being in politics is like being a football coach. You have to be smart enough to understand the game, and dumb enough to think it's important."

—EUGENE MCCARTHY

✦✦✦

Q: Why do only 15 percent of politicians get into heaven?
A: If it were more, it would be hell.

True or False: The Politician Sex Scandal Edition

Read the following scenarios and decide for yourself if it is true or false.

1. A video went viral showing Congressman Madison Cawthorn naked in bed with another man, thrusting his genitals in the man's face. The congressman said the video was made years ago when he was being crass with a friend.

    ✦✦✦

2. The Department of Justice investigated Congressman Matt Gaetz for violated federal sex trafficking laws.

3. Congresswoman Katie Hill was alleged to have engaged in an extramarital affair with a male legislative director as well as a female staffer.

♦♦♦

4. Congressman Bob Barr introduced the "Defense of Marriage" act—and was subsequently photographed licking whipped cream off strippers at his inaugural party.

♦♦♦

5. 5. While married—to President Johnson's daughter, no less—Senator Charles Robb was alleged to have received a nude massage from Miss Virginia. Was there a happy ending?

6. Congressman Georg Santos faces charges of stealing money from a GoFundMe campaign for a disabled veteran's dying service dog; lying about his mother being in New York during the 9/11 attacks; embellishing his resume; lying about his professional background; lying about his heritage; lying about his assets; lying about his grandparents fleeing Nazis; and being involved in a check fraud case in Brazil.

♦♦♦

7. Senator John Ensign had an affair with a close friend and staffer (whose husband also worked for him) that was disclosed at his own Fox News press conference.

♦♦♦

8. Once a VP hopeful, John Edwards fell for a filmmaker who he hired to cover his campaign, fathered her child, and used campaign funds to hide it all. The trifecta.

9. Congressman Wilbur Mills was discovered drunk and beaten up, in the company of an Argentinian stripper, with whom he was having an affair. He didn't resign until giving a drunk press conference from a burlesque house dressing room.

•••

10. Congresswoman Lauren Boebert was escorted out of a performance of *Beetlejuice* for vaping in her seat, taking selfies during the performance, and touching her date inappropriately while he touched her.

•••

Answers: 1–10: True

"A good politician is quite as unthinkable as an honest burglar."

—H. L. MENCKEN

"In a closed society where everybody's guilty, the only crime is getting caught. In a world of thieves, the only final sin is stupidity."

—HUNTER S. THOMPSON

•••

Asked if he prayed for the senators when he served as the Senate chaplain, Edward Everett Hale replied, "No. I look at the senators and pray for the country."

CHAPTER ELEVEN:

The Snark hall of Fame

Whew, we're nearing the end. While researching this book, we've come across snark that was above and beyond normal snark. It was supersized. We collected it all and put it here at the end, just to make sure you're still paying attention. From the snarkiest people to ever grace this world to awesomely wonderful ways to die and talk about the dead, this chapter has it all.

When You Hate Everyone and You Know It, Clap Your Hands!

A misanthrope is a person who hates or distrusts humankind . . . also known as a realist. We here feel that people are good and fine and wonderful, as long as you don't get to know them. If you are a misanthrope, here are some T-shirt messages for you.

There are two different types of people in this world, and I hate both of them.

•••

"I am free of all prejudice. I hate everyone equally."
—W. C. Fields

"Think of how stupid the average person is, and realize half of them are stupider than that."
—George Carlin

"I don't hate [people]. I just feel better when they are not around."

—CHARLES BUKOWSKI

◆◆◆

"I'm tire of this back-slappin' 'isn't humanity neat' bullshit. We're a virus with shoes."
—BILL HICKS

◆◆◆

"What is Man? A miserable little pile of secrets."
—ANDRÉ MALRAUX

For me, to be human is, for the most part, to hate what I am. When I suddenly realize that I am one of them, I want to scream in horror."

—ROBERT CRUMB

◆◆◆

"If everything seems to be going well, you have obviously overlooked something."
—STEVEN WRIGHT

◆◆◆

Q: How often do planes crash?
A: Once.

Inspirational Quotes for Realistic People

Reading inspirational quotes is like looking at your gym membership card to lose weight. Not only are they useless, but quite frankly, if you post more than one inspirational post a week, we actually start worrying about your mental health. Remember: You are only as deep as your most recently posted inspirational quote!

෴

Be yourself . . . no, not your real self. No one wants to see that shit.

♦♦♦

Someone out there is thinking of you. It's not me, though. I think you're an asshole.

♦♦♦

Be the reason someone smiles today . . . or drinks.

The path to peace begins with four simple words: not my fucking problem.

✦✦✦

Money Cannot Buy Happiness . . . although I have a receipt from the liquor store that tells a whole different story.

✦✦✦

Follow your heart, unless that asshole is giving out bad directions.

✦✦✦

Don't judge someone by their appearance. Judge them for the little shit they are on the inside.

✦✦✦

Wherever you go, there you are . . . being an asshole again.

✦✦✦

Aging gracefully is an art. Aging disgracefully is a fucking blast.

Bless me with the courage to know what I cannot change. And to know when it's time to fuck some things up.

◆◆◆

Silence is golden. Duct tape is silver.

◆◆◆

Life is good, you should get one.

◆◆◆

There are plenty of fish in the ocean. Too bad they're all swimming away from you.

◆◆◆

Everything happens for no reason. Or: Everything happens for a reason. Today, the reason could be that you're a dick.

◆◆◆

If at first, you don't succeed, skydiving is not for you.

◆◆◆

Give a man a fish and he eats for a day.

Dear . . .

Think of this last "Dear" section as sticky notes for stupid people. Leave one of these thoughtful notes on a computer screen, refrigerator, bedroom door, or car windshield. The stupid people will appreciate the thought you put into carefully crafting your note, and will kindly take your advice. For reals.

∽

Smart Ass at the Grocery Store Who Counted My Groceries,

Yeah, I'm in the express lane with eleven items, but two peanut butters count as one so if you're going to be a smart ass, first make sure that you're smart.

♦♦♦

Person Whose Car Just Got Hit by a Cart in the Target Parking Lot,

I see the fuck-up fairy has visited us again.

Person Who Royally Fucked Up the Big Sales Presentation at Work,

People like you are the reason God doesn't talk to us anymore.

◆◆◆

Person Who Keeps Looking at Me Funny When I Try for the Fourth Time to Explain How Apple Pay Works,

I don't have the time or the crayons to explain this to you.

◆◆◆

Person Who Thinks I Like Them,

Just because I'm smiling doesn't mean I like you. I might be picturing you on fire.

◆◆◆

You can't fix stupid, but you can unsubscribe from their updates.

Karma's just sharpening her nails and finishing her drink. She says she'll be with you shortly.

···

Teach a man to fish, and you're stuck fishing with some guy you barely know.

···

"There is no sunrise so beautiful that it is worth waking me up to see it."

—MINDY KALING

Snark Hall of Fame: The Snarkiest Mother Fuckers in the World

These snarky fuckers get a whole section to themselves. These folks are known for their snark almost as much or more than what they actually did for a living.

〜

"Some cause happiness wherever they go; others whenever they go."
—OSCAR WILDE

"Tell him I've been too fucking busy—or vice versa."
—DOROTHY PARKER

•••

"Whatever you do, always give 100 percent. Unless you're donating blood."
—BILL MURRAY

From a review of A.A. Milne's *The House at Pooh Corner*: "And it is that word 'hummy' my darlings, that marks the first place in *The House at Pooh Corner* at which Tonstant Weader Fwowed up."
—Dorothy Parker

♦♦♦

"Tact is the ability to tell someone to go to hell in such a way that they look forward to the journey."
—Winston Churchill

"Behind every successful man is a woman. Behind her is his wife."
—Groucho Marx

♦♦♦

"Only dull people are brilliant at breakfast."
—Oscar Wilde

♦♦♦

"Never be afraid to laugh at yourself, after all, you could be missing out on the joke of the century."
—Joan Rivers

"I've had a perfectly wonderful evening. But this wasn't it."
—GROUCHO MARX

•••

"Light travels faster than sound. This is why some people appear bright until they speak."
—STEVEN WRIGHT

•••

"Everybody knows how to raise children, except the people who have them."
—P.J. O'ROURKE

"God gave men both a penis and a brain, but unfortunately not enough blood supply to run both at the same time."
—ROBIN WILLIAMS

•••

"My doctor gave me six months to live, but when I couldn't pay the bill he gave me six months more."
—WALTER MATTHAU

Snarky Superpowers

Sure, we all want to fly and burn shit with our eyes—but we can't, and that sucks. We can, however, hone our snarky superpowers. Here are but a few:

With a mere head shake, I can make any employee I work alongside realize that talking to me this early in the day before I've had my damn coffee is not on the table.

✦✦✦

I tell you to stop talking . . . and you do.

✦✦✦

I have special vision that tells me if you are always this stupid or if it's a special occasion.

✦✦✦

My voice brings home the point that I'm not insulting you; I'm merely describing you.

Like a sixth sense, I can call bullshit and be right 100 percent of the time.

◆◆◆

I gain a time refund on any time I've invested on people who weren't worth it.

◆◆◆

My autocorrect never thinks I'm saying "shot" when I mean "shit." Or "fork" . . . well, you get the idea.

◆◆◆

I blink, and you go away.

"Everything happens for a reason. Sometimes the reason is that you're stupid and make bad decisions."

—Marion G. Harmon

Sick Burns Hall of Fame

You look good for someone your age.

◆◆◆

You didn't fall from the stupid tree. You were dragged through the whole dumbass forest.

◆◆◆

Your flexibility amazes me. How do you get your foot in your mouth and your head up your ass at the same time?

◆◆◆

You look like I need a drink.

◆◆◆

You're impossible to underestimate.

◆◆◆

Orgasms are one of the healthiest forms of stress release. So when I tell you to go fuck yourself, I'm just letting you know I care.

I told my therapist about you.

◆◆◆

To this day, that bully from school still takes my lunch money. He makes a great Subway sandwich.

◆◆◆

Someday you'll go far. When you do, I hope you stay there.

◆◆◆

I'll never forget the first day we met . . . no matter how hard I try.

◆◆◆

You're not stupid! You just have bad luck when you're thinking.

Life Hacks

Here are some great ways to get through the day when you want to punch life right in its face!

1. Buy a really nice TV and put the box by your neighbor's trash so you don't get robbed. And if your neighbor gets robbed? Fuck 'em!

2. Sleep till noon so you only have to eat two meals a day. Fuck breakfast—am I right?!

3. Cooking kale? Use a lot of olive oil so it's easier to scrape that shit in the garbage.

4. Money tight? No worries. Just don't tell your three-year-old it's her birthday.

5. Ice-maker broken? Use frozen vegetables in your drinks.

6. Wearing dirty clothes? Rub a dryer sheet on yourself.

7. Participating in behavior you will regret in the morning? See #2.

8. Be the piece of shit you want to be—not the one everyone thinks you are.
9. It takes thirty-seven muscles to frown, but zero muscles to not give a shit.
10. Phone battery dying all the time? Put it the fuck down once or twice a day.

Have a nice day. Somewhere else.

♦♦♦

Everyone's entitled to make mistakes around here, but you're abusing the privilege.

♦♦♦

I'm not saying I hate you, all I'm saying is that you are literally the Monday of my life.

♦♦♦

"The only reason some people get lost in thought is that it's an unfamiliar territory."

—Paul Fix

Road Snark

Road snark is defined as road rage that is so much better for your health. In other words, these this is road rage with the windows closed, whispering, while squeezing the steering wheel as if your choking someone to death.

Match the driving offense to the road rage comment.

A. The driver who is going too slow

B. The driver in the middle of the road

C. The driver who doesn't signal a turn

D. The driver with 17 peace sign bumper stickers

E. The driver who tailgates you in the fast lane even though you're going 15 miles over the speed limit and then gets pulled over by a cop.

F. The driver in the pick-up weaving in and out of traffic

G. The driver texting when the light turns.

♦♦♦

1. Didn't realize turn signals were optional now.
2. Pick a fucking lane, jack wagon!
3. The gas pedal's on the right, asswipe.
4. Not only are your opinions shit, but you drive like a dead hippie.
5. Let me spell "schadenfreude" for you.
6. Green is for go, fuckwad.
7. Are you just doing that so your truck nuts get some air?

◆◆◆

Answers: A. 3; B. 2; C. 1; D. 4; E. 5; F. 8; G. 7

___

"According to most studies, people's number one fear is public speaking. Number two is death. Death is number two! Does that sound right? This means to the average person, if you go to a funeral, you're better off in the casket than doing the eulogy."
—JERRY SEINFELD

One Last Crack Before I Go . . .

There are few things more satisfying than being able to say something clever, cutting, and crass right before you croak. Can you match the person to his or her final words?

∽

A. Louis B. Mayer
B. Lady Nancy Astor
C. Carl Panzram
D. Humphrey Bogart
E. James W. Rodgers
F. Winston Churchill

•••

1. I should never have switched from Scotch to martinis.
2. I'm bored with it all.
3. Hurry it up, you Hoosier bastard! I could hang a dozen men while you're screwing around.

4. Am I dying, or is this my birthday?
5. It wasn't worth it.
6. A bulletproof vest. (Asked if he has any last requests before facing a firing squad.)

♦♦♦

Answers: 1. D.; 2. F.; 3. C.; 4. B.; 5. A.; 6. E.

"I have never killed a man, but I have read many obituaries with great pleasure."
—CLARENCE DARROW

♦♦♦

You can't spell "funeral" without "fun."

♦♦♦

"Amazing tradition. They throw a great party for you on the one day they know you can't come."
—JEFF GOLDBLUM

Snarky Ways to Begin a Eulogy

As we near the end of this book, let's contemplate the real end of the "book," so to speak. When you find yourself in a position of eulogizing a loved one (or not so loved one) consider the following . . . and then say something else entirely.

∽

So, who else was written out of the will?

✦✦✦

Looks like I won the time-of-death pool.

✦✦✦

Next time someone says, "Call a doctor," I won't assume it's a joke.

✦✦✦

This really doesn't surprise me in a family that considers *Goodfellas* a date film.

I guess that was the main circuit breaker after all.

+++

I bet you $100 he isn't in there.

+++

Before I begin, help me answer this question: Does a eulogy have to be nice?

+++

Hold on, this call's important.

+++

If anyone sees a lost flip-flop, it's probably mine.

+++

Please hold the applause until the end.

+++

Old people at weddings always poke me and say, "You're next!" So I started doing the same thing to them at funerals.

Rest in Pieces

The only thing better than having cool last words, is to get in one last snarky jibe by having it engraved for all time on your tombstone. Start thinking of your own snarky epitaph now, before it's too late.

Where his soul's gone or how it fares; nobody knows, and nobody cares.
—ANONYMOUS

•••

Hotten Rotten Forgotten
—John Hotten

•••

"He is useless on top of the ground; he ought to be under it, inspiring the cabbages."
—MARK TWAIN

Here lies one whose name was writ in water.
—John Keats

•••

Called back.
—EMILY DICKINSON

•••

Excuse my dust.
—Dorothy Parker

•••

"On my gravestone, I want it to say, 'I told you I was sick.'"
—Tom Waits

CONCLUSION

*A*nd in the end, the snark you take is equal to the snark you make.

Those are the words I ended my first book (*The Snark Handbook: A Reference Guide to Verbal Sparring*) with, taking Paul McCartney's existentialist poetry and pompously changing the words . . . and haven't heard a word from the remaining fabs yet. Why haven't I? Fear of snark.

Snark is a tool. Yes, the ability to snark can change your life. (Not really, but it looks good as I type it out on the computer.) It can diffuse a tense situation, or it can "fuse" one. Your choice.

All you need to do is follow a few simple rules:

1. Snark fast. When the opportunity presents itself, jump in.
2. Snark hard. Pull no punches.
3. Snark last. The final word is the best word.

And when these few rules fail, follow the advice of Teddy Roosevelt and carry a big stick.

Stay snarky.

—LD